BITTERSWEET

The Life and Struggles of a Bipolar

BITTERSWEET

The Life and Struggles of a Bipolar

By Gladys J. Seedorf, LCSW

SEEDORF BOOK PUBLISHING
BATTLE CREEK, MICHIGAN

BITTERSWEET
The Life and Struggles of a Bipolar

Published by Seedorf Book Publishing
11135 Burrows Road
Battle Creek, MI 49014
(269) 425-8747
g01131963@yahoo.com

Gladys Seedorf, Publisher
Yvonne Rose, Book Packager (www.qualitypress.info)
Printed Page, Interior and Cover Design

ISBN 978-0-9892590-9-5
Library of Congress Control Number: 2015905446

In Memory of Louis Peterson
April 1, 1932 - November 9, 2012

Dedication

I dedicate this book to my daughter, Monique, my sister, Linda Lovelace, and her three children, Jaquita, Barongiere, and Darrington

Thanks & Acknowledgements

I would like to thank my dear husband James for his awesome support and for his many kind words of encouragement. He is simply a wonderful husband and father. He never hesitates to jump in and lend a helping hand or just sit patiently while listening to my ongoing thoughts and ideas. After thirty years of marriage, he still treats me like a very delicate rose. I will never forget the very important advice that he has given me over the years and that has served me well… "Gladys, don't ever become so busy that you forget to enjoy life, regardless of the bad times, there will always be sunny days ahead, and if all else fails please read the directions!" Thank you so much my sweet love.

A very special thank you goes to my two special daughters, Danielle and Monique, for all of their time and patience as well. I'm so very proud of them for being such nice young ladies.

Bushels of roses go to my mother, Willie Jewel Peterson for being such a great inspiration to me for instilling not only her words of wisdom but also for passing on such a very sweet and gentle spirit. She has a wonderful appreciation for life's most simple pleasures that always seem to allow her to somehow find peace in the midst of adversity, comfort in the warmth of the sun, joy in the sound of singing birds, and even humor in her own errors. I definitely thank her for not only teaching, but showing me how to roll up my sleeves and work hard for the things that I desired and not expect that anything would be handed to me without first delaying gratification. Most important, she showed me how to get down on my knees and pray on a daily basis rather than wait until a crisis arose. Mama said, "You ought to always stay prayed up." In doing so, I found it much easier to emulate her by taking God by the right hand and walking through my journey of life.

A special note of thanks goes out to my dear friend Karin DeGraw, for unselfishly sharing all of her priceless book writing expertise with me. Karen has always had a very soft and unspoken way of letting me know that perhaps I may need to rethink some things. Though I often laugh, I greatly value her friendship and consider myself very fortunate to have had the pleasure of working with her for almost nine years. Thank you for bringing sunshine into my work days.

I certainly don't want to forget my dear neighbors: Clint and Kim Johnson, Roger and Yvonne Thomson, George and Jeannette Martin, and Martha McMillan Purvis who have all been genuinely kind and very supportive to me as well. I must not fail to mention, that Martha is extremely talented; she makes the most beautiful quilts and frequently avails herself to me to share her talent. Truly I consider all these people to be such a great blessing to me and my family. It is a pleasure to spend time with them and, without a doubt, I know for sure that I have the best neighbors that anyone could have.

Another special note of thanks goes out to my two wonderful friends at Southern Exposure Herb Farm, Curtis Whitaker and Scott Stokes. When I think of Curtis and Scott, I am reminded of Maya Angelou's words, "People may not always remember what you say, but they will always remember how you made them feel." I feel that they both have a heart of gold, which I have found to be extremely radiant. I've observed them on many occasions go above and beyond the call of duty to help others, not to mention the fact that they have been very supportive of me as well. I also feel that our friendship has blossomed into something really beautiful and I am so humbled by it. I consider Curtis and Scott to be part of my family and there will always be a special place in my heart for them. Hugs and love to both of you!

Another sweet and dear friend of mine is Ella Mae Hoyt-Tony. Not only has Ella Mae been a good friend, but also her family. She has blessed me and my family with such amazing magnanimous generosity. There is a very sweet and gentle spirit that flows like a river through this family and obviously begins with Ella Mae. It has truly been a pleasure getting to know everyone and reaping the benefits from being part of such a wonderful family. I definitely treasure the time I spend with Ella Mae and her family.

I thank Tony and Yvonne Rose, Directors of Quality Press, for their expertise and advice. You've both been extremely helpful and your feedback is always welcome.

To my favorite cousin, James E. Dunklin who recently passed away. I will never forget him for his sincere altruistic personality. During the times that he spent doing for others, I believe he was truly in his comfort zone. James wanted to help people regardless of the fact that he may or may not be paid. I often referred to him as the Jack of all trades. If he didn't know how to complete a task, he wouldn't rest until he found out. As I look around my house, both inside and out, I still admire all of his wonderful craftsmanship. James was also an excellent southern cook who definitely knew his way around in the kitchen. He always walked around with a big smile on his face and a very contagious laugh that I can still hear. It was literally impossible to be in a room with him and come out without feeling such a magnitude of sunshine and warmth that only he could emit. I miss you my dear cousin, but more, I look forward to seeing you in heaven.

I would even like to thank my father, the late Louis Peterson, who definitely played a major role in my upbringing by setting the best possible example, based upon his circumstances. I have learned a great deal from his life and also from his death. I am certain that he would be proud to know that I took the time to unravel and understand his mental health issues, which so greatly impacted him and the family. Had it not been for his tumultuous journey through life, I am certain that I would not have chosen to explore his particular mental health issues. To honor his life, I and the family have decided to set up a scholarship memorial to benefit those individuals who struggle with mental health issues and who would like to further their education.

Last but not least, I thank and praise God for not only breathing precious life into me, but more for bestowing such marvelous gifts of health and strength, which I do not take for granted and vow to use them every day to make the lives of others a bit easier. I am certain that these are precious gifts and not simply an entitlement that I have earned or much less deserve. Just as sure as the sun rises in the morning and sets in the evening; and regardless of my thoughts or feelings, I know that I have absolutely nothing to complain about, but yet everything to be grateful for because I am truly blessed beyond measure. God, you are so amazing. You have richly blessed me by surrounding me with a host of genuinely kind and caring people who are like an enormous bouquet of flowers that I will carry in my heart for the rest of my life. Surely this is more valuable than anything else I could have ever asked for. God I love you and adore you… Hallelujah!

Lilly's Prayer

Lawd, I sho wanna thank you for watchin over me and my family late in the midnight hours while I slumba and sleep, not knowin nothin about myself. You have abled me to rise up in due time wit the blood still runnin wom in my veins, activity in my limbs and clothed in my right mind. After findin me truly saved and sanctified and filled wit the precious Holy Ghost, I'm askin prayars of the righteous to pray much for me that I will be the daughta that you is callin on in these last and evil days.

In yo name, Lawd Jesus, Amen and Amen.

Table of Contents

PART ONE

Getting to Know Joe

Chapter One

Honey Dun Gone On In

On November 9, 2012, around 8:00 p.m., Denise phoned Carolyn on her cell phone and asked if she was sitting down. "Well, yes, I'm just driving home from a movie," she said. Carolyn could tell by the tone of her voice that it was something serious.

"Call me back when you get home," Denise said.

"Okay I'll be home in just a few minutes," she responded. Carolyn had a gut feeling that it had something to do with her father Joe, but she prayed that it was something else. Shortly after arriving home, she returned the call only to be told that her father had died.

"I've asked that the body not be moved until we arrive. How soon can you meet me there?" Denise asked.

"I'll leave right now, I should be there within two hours," said Carolyn.

The ride to the nursing home seemed as if it would never end. The drive took longer than usual because the roads were a bit slippery from the snow. At 10:00 p.m., two sisters, Carolyn who was the youngest, Denise, and their mother, Lilly, arrived at the nursing home. They were met at the door by several anxiously awaiting staff who led them down a very long, dark and quiet corridor. The walk seemed like an eternity. The mere thought of knowing that they would soon view the body of their deceased loved one Joe, made them feel completely numb inside.

"I really feel like crying, but I just can't," said Carolyn.

By this time all of the residents were nestled in bed and asleep for the night. Other than the staff, there was no sign of life. As they approached the room, the aides began to express condolences. They reported that Joe had been fairly active during the day, but was later found slumped over in his wheelchair by the aide who delivered his dinner. Of course the family knew that his health had declined, but they were stunned by the news of his sudden death.

As they arrived in the room, the curtain was drawn and the light was on. They gently pulled back the curtain and found him sleeping peacefully as if he was just taking a short nap. The atmosphere was very quiet and serene; his sleep appeared to be very sweet. Joe looked as though he had not a care in the world. His arms were folded as normal when he slept. By this time his body temperature was as cold as ice, but Carolyn kneeled to kiss his forehead, which was very unusual for her since this was certainly nothing that he ever welcomed. As they viewed the body, they noticed that he had recently received a very clean haircut and shave, almost as if it was for this special occasion.

"You know, he looks really good. I don't think I ever saw him look so calm and relaxed," said Denise. His face looked as if it bore just a hint of a smile.

"Honey done gone on in," said Lilly. She seemed somewhat relieved that Joe, her ex-spouse was deceased because she knew that he had been ill and at least his suffering was over. Even though Joe and Lilly had been divorced for three years, she continued to refer to him as "honey." Although he was eighty years old, his skin appeared as if he was barely forty. He no longer had the sour look of depression, stress, or anxiety on his face. In addition to his physical illnesses, he also endured quite a combination of mental illnesses and addictions that essentially plagued and robbed him of enjoying life with his family and friends. As they looked at him, it was obvious that all those dreadful wicked illnesses no longer held him captive. Everyone agreed that his purpose on this earth was finished and that perhaps God had dispatched the Angel of Death to not only relieve him of all earthly duties, but also to rescue him from a host of illnesses.

"Maybe now he can be happy because he's no longer trapped inside his body," said Carolyn.

"I don't know, but I sure hope so because he just couldn't seem to find happiness, nor did he seem to want anybody else to be happy either," said Denise.

"A thought comes to mind and I am reminded of the story in the Bible, (Mark 5:1-20) when Jesus healed the Demon possessed man by commanding the Legion of demons to come out of him," said Carolyn.

Joe frequently exhibited severe mood swings, bouts of paranoia, narcissistic and antisocial behaviors, depression, anxiety, agitation, and even perhaps a degree of Schizophrenia. Because he had such a plethora of mental illnesses, he undoubtedly had an awful time trying to maneuver through life. Nevertheless, he functioned as best he could, based on the hand of life that was dealt to him. Naturally, he felt more comfortable being alone because he appeared to be more content and less agitated. He worked hard to avoid a lot of stimulation, large crowds, etc. Of course, he would never admit that he had a problem or take medication for it and like most people, he swore that everyone else had the problem.

"Indeed he had a Cross to bear that he did not ask for, but I still like to think that God blessed him with a wonderful companion to at least soften the blow, even if he wasn't able to comprehend it," said Denise.

Joe was born on April 1, 1932 in Malone, Florida in a barn. He was very sick as a child. His parents were impoverished farmers and struggled to make ends meet, which was pretty typical for most black families at that time. Nobody had much of anything, according to Lilly. To make matters worse, Joe frequently mentioned that his dad left his mother when he was a child and never came back. Being the only male, he was devastated and vowed that he would never do such a thing to his family. Consequently, his grandparents raised him and his three sisters, in order for his mother to seek employment. On several occasions, he jokingly said that his grandparents sometimes whipped him for no reason. He often recalled one instance when he was sitting on the floor playing and his grandmother ran up behind and held him upside down by the leg while she whipped him. Although Joe never acknowledged this, some of his family members indicated that he was indeed bullied by other school age children. It was apparent that he didn't feel good about his childhood because he never had anything positive to say.

Joe also mentioned that he wasn't allowed to go to school regularly because he was needed at home to work the farm, but for some reason his grandparents thought it was important to send his sisters. Finally after so many years had gone by, the State laws changed and mandated all children to attend school. Joe was then allowed to go, but by that time, he was so academically challenged that he couldn't keep up. He was an older student that was placed in a classroom with much younger children. Obviously the teachers had a difficult time because he needed more help than they could provide.

Needless to say, he was very discouraged, embarrassed and eventually dropped out of school and sought employment. As time went on, he was old enough to leave home. Joe once said that he was interested in serving in the Military Armed Forces, but was denied due to illiteracy. Consequently, he found work doing odd jobs such as: picking cotton, plucking and wringing the necks off of chickens, working in factories, and as a golf caddy. As a young man, he became a habitual smoker and drinker, but fortunately always managed to go to work, whenever it was available. Although he made very little money, he always had some type of old car to drive around.

Chapter Two

The Union of Joe and Lilly

While living in Pensacola, Florida, Joe met and eventually married Lilly in 1956. Following the marriage, they moved to Cambridge, Maryland in search of steady employment. Now Lilly was a very devout Christian and just felt that it was time to be married. As a young lady, Lilly had never lived alone. She left her parents' home, which was in Greenville, Alabama, and later moved in with her uncle who owned a small grocery store in Pensacola, Florida.

During her era, it was improper for a man and woman to live together and/or date for long periods. Lilly wanted to be a good Christian and marry Joe, without delay. Of course she loved him, or at least she thought so. The marriage produced three beautiful children. The first child died of pneumonia, which was accompanied by severe diarrhea at the age of four months. Of course, both Lilly and Joe were devastated. Lilly blamed the fact that money was so terribly scarce and the apartment they lived in was nothing more than a poorly insulated shack. "The po chile couldn't keep wom, and yo daddy wouldn't let me put her in na bed wit us," Lilly said.

Lilly and Joe arranged to have an extremely meager funeral, since neither of them had much money. The headstone at the cemetery was just a thin slab of cement, on which someone actually wrote the date of their baby's birth and death. This was a very emotionally draining time for both of them. From that day forward, Lilly vowed that any more babies would sleep in the bed with them, so she could assure that they kept warm.

Since Joe's employment was scanty, he had no issue with staying home babysitting the children while Lilly went to work. Likewise, Lilly felt that Joe was nice to the children and could save money by taking care of them.

There was one time, in particular, that Joe had a problem; but he called Lilly at work and insisted that she come home right away. Joe said that he had just made a fresh pot of coffee and poured himself a cup when curious baby Carolyn, who had just started walking, managed to waddle up to the table and pull it onto herself. By the time Lilly arrived home, Joe was frantic and Carolyn screamed hysterically as the coffee had burned the skin right off her arm. Of course Lilly knew just what to do. She rubbed some salve on her arm and immediately took her to the doctor. Joe felt terrible, but Lilly comforted him as well.

Since there was no freezer in the apartment, they used the window sills to keep food cold. In spite of the fact that the living situation was absolute penury, Lilly dearly loved her husband and babies and she was determined to make the best of a bad situation. She continued to work at the local sewing factory doing "piece work" which meant she was paid based on the number of pieces she sewed. Since money was scarce Lilly always walked to work each day and by the end of the day she was so utterly exhausted that she would take a cab home.

After about two years she came to the conclusion that she wanted a different kind of life. Not only did she want prosperity, but she desperately wanted her husband to have a steady job instead of scanty low pay employment. Lilly also mentioned that she was tired of constantly watching Joe borrow money from his mother that she knew he couldn't afford to repay, and to make matters worse, she was tired of hearing his mother tell him "no." She saw her life as no more than a dead end street but she was determined to break free and forge ahead. Lilly always imagined that she would someday own a home and have the financial stability to send her children to college. "I'm gone move to Michigan wit my sista Bessie Mae and you can either come wit me or you can stay here," she told Joe. Lilly didn't know what was ahead, but she knew what she actually had and that she wanted no more of it.

Now Joe was no fool, he always said, "I might look like a fool, but I ain't nobody's fool." He wasn't about to let his wife leave and take his kids out of state without him. After all, he knew she wouldn't be coming back. Without any hesitation, he packed up their few belongings and the family headed to Michigan. The move was especially difficult because money was scarce. Although Bessie Mae and her husband also had meager jobs, it was still more than Joe and Lilly had. Bessie Mae didn't hesitate to encourage and welcome Lilly and her family to her home in Michigan. Lilly's plan was to move in with her sister, at least until she and Joe could find employment. Unfortunately the old saying held true… "If it weren't for bad luck, they would have no luck at all."

Almost immediately following the move (1965) the situation grew worse as yet another child, baby Carolyn, was hospitalized and near death due to pneumonia. Lilly kept asking Dr. Ralph "is my baby gone make it thew da night?" but he would make no promises and shook his head saying, "I don't know, we'll just have to wait until tomorrow." Although Lilly had very little money to pay the doctor, she had a ton of faith, hope, and prayers that she lived by. As time went on, baby Carolyn's health slowly improved and once again, God answered Lilly's prayers.

The worst news was yet to come. Following a brief illness, Bessie Mae died. It seemed that Lilly's support group slipped away, just as fast as she found it. Nevertheless, Lilly was determined to try to make a life for her family. By this time, she and Joe had moved into their own apartment and found jobs that they felt would at least make ends meet.

The fact that Joe drank and smoked had no effect on Lilly because she took her wedding vows seriously. As a matter of fact, Lilly said, "Don't worry bout it, cause you will stop after a while." Unbeknownst to Lilly this would truly be the very least of her worries. Surprisingly, about ten years later, Joe actually did stop smoking without any withdrawal and or relapse. Carolyn said, "I remember the day he came home from work and said he only had a half pack of Lucky Strike cigarettes left over in his pocket, but decided to throw them away because he simply no longer enjoyed the taste."

Joe said that he had originally planned to stop smoking after he finished this last pack, but could see no sense in waiting.

"I never saw him smoke past that day, nor have I seen him buy or make any cigarettes either," said Denise.

Now this tickled Lilly to no end and she felt pretty proud of her prediction, but little did she know that her marriage was about to take an extremely turbulent journey. Lilly certainly didn't know anything about any mental illnesses or personality disorders, but she was well aware of the fact that Joe's personality seemed to change, within an instant, with very little to no warning. Since Lilly was usually very busy and a hard worker, she never thought much of it. She certainly wasn't afraid of him, but she undoubtedly knew he was irascible. Lilly was very cautious and at all cost avoided bringing up subjects that she knew would upset him. As the marriage progressed, so did the verbal abuse. As far as his outbursts were concerned, she just felt that she often took the brunt of his anger that actually should have been directed towards someone else. Lilly was very gentle and kind and truly didn't believe in holding a grudge, so she always carried on as if nothing ever happened.

Years later, before either of the girls left home for college, Carolyn felt that something just wasn't right with Joe. She said, "Something just isn't right with him, I just cannot put my finger on it." While in college, she took a couple of beginner's psychology classes and was able to learn a bit more about personality disorders and mental illnesses. She couldn't quite diagnose him, but to the best of her ability he suffered from many illnesses on any given day.

The term "mental illness" was certainly nothing that Joe was accustomed to hearing, let alone seek medical advice for. Joe and Lilly rarely had enough money to pay their bills, let alone have him go to the doctor to report that he felt angry about something, which he always insisted was caused by someone else.

Because the lack of money was always an issue, nobody ever went to the doctor unless they could actually see blood. Lilly frequently said, "you be auight, go get you a couple of aspirins." There were always aspirin in the house to take before any doctor appointments were made.

Although Joe was never professionally diagnosed, based on Carolyn's level of expertise, he had severe Bipolar symptoms. Joe was extremely manipulative and refused to ever accept blame for anything, unless it was good; and even if nobody else was involved, he somehow found a way to blame others for his misfortunes. Of course, he never had any difficulty taking credit for anything that Lilly spearheaded, especially if it had a positive outcome; but yet he wasn't about to give her a compliment either. As a matter of fact, nobody ever heard him give anybody a compliment, because it just wasn't part of his personality. He often exhibited very severe mood swings. One minute he was just fine, and the next he was as angry as an erupting volcano. After a while, the girls could sense when the physical violence would occur because the look on Joe's face changed drastically. All of a sudden his eyes widened, he began grinding his false teeth, and you could cut the tension in the room with a knife.

"When the hairs on my neck stood up and my heart began to race, I always knew what was about to follow," said Carolyn. Following a very brief period of silence, malaise entered the room and all hell broke loose. "I honestly think he became temporarily insane," said Carolyn.

"Me too," said Denise. Joe would run through the house like a tornado, physically beating Lilly and the girls with his belt while he yelled and cussed like a sailor. He had such a malevolent look on his face while he violently swung his leather belt that always left big bloody welts, wherever the belt managed to land. Joe always wore an old worn out black leather belt which he abruptly removed in what seemed like a split second. "I can still hear the sound that the leather belt made as he hit us on our backs over and over until we cried," said Denise. "Swish, swoosh."

"Sometimes I would cry before actually being hit because I would anticipate the pain of the belt and I hoped that he would feel sorry for me and change his mind, but that never happened." said Carolyn.

Of course Lilly would try to defend them if she felt he was being too brash with them. "Leave my kids lone," she said. Usually it did no good and only made matters worse because he wouldn't hesitate to punch, slap, and kick her as well. When Joe realized that everyone was terribly frightened and as helpless as could be, his anger would subside. Following his horrific explosion, Lilly and the girls did their best to put the house and themselves back together. Of course some objects could not be repaired.

As children, both Carolyn and Denise had terribly low self-esteem, which they described as being lower than the basement. Regrettably, Carolyn developed a nervous issue as a result of his abuse. The combination of witnessing and being a part of so much violence almost silenced her.

Because she was so nervous and withdrawn as a child, she had a difficult time in school. Sadly, Carolyn's third grade teacher, Mrs. Felton, was no help at all and was often part of the problem because she too was verbally and physically abusive to the children. Since there were no laws against teachers whipping the children, Mrs. Felton never hesitated to grab a child and literally shake him or her senseless, and or use her yard stick to beat the poor child into a daze. Now she never actually touched Carolyn, but her famous words to her were, "you do poorly at your best." Carolyn never forgot those very hurtful and discouraging words that definitely required an emotional band aid. Because Carolyn frequently cried for no reason, she was also ridiculed by the other children. There were times that she didn't want to be at school, and Lord knows she didn't want to be at home either. "I just remember feeling very nervous and scared and if anyone stared at me too long, I assumed that something was wrong," said Carolyn.

Sometimes Mrs. Felton would call home in an attempt to gain insight as to what the problems were, but neither Joe nor Lilly were patient with Carolyn. In retrospect, Lilly did the best she could, but she worked full time and Lord knows she had her hands full trying to deal with Joe from day to day. Lilly's advice to Carolyn was "Put yo feelins in yo pocket and don't let nobody know they dun hurt yo feelins."

Many years later Carolyn was informed by one of her classmates that Mrs. Felton had died. "Maybe God decided to spare other kids from her wretched abuse," Carolyn said in a rather cheerful tone. The fact that Mrs. Felton's husband was the Pastor of one of the local churches absolutely astonished Carolyn. She felt that he would have been shocked if he really knew how abusive Mrs. Felton was to the children, but perhaps he did. Now Mrs. Felton and her spouse had adopted three children, none of which seemed to be very happy in Carolyn's opinion. Maybe she was just as abusive to her own children as well.

Chapter Three

Patterns of Violent Episodes

In spite of Joe's abusive personality, he did have at least one great asset. He had a wonderful set of lungs that allowed him to yell and scream loud enough to shake you to the core. Not even Tarzan could compete with Joe. "Sometimes he yelled so loud that I actually wet my pants," said Denise.

Now Lilly never said she wet her pants, but she was assuredly startled by his sudden screams, as well. Joe often yelled and screamed as a way to intimidate Lilly, but he wouldn't hesitate to physically abuse her if she disagreed or challenged him on a topic that he felt was important. In fact, it seemed to make him feel rather powerful, knowing that he could dominate the family any time he wanted. Sometimes if she was lucky, she could diffuse the situation by remaining silent and not respond to his accusations, but on the other hand, Joe was irascible and would become violently angry if she refused to respond, especially if his intentions were to pick a fight. She was damned if she did and she was damned if she didn't. Following a violent episode he never bothered to express compassion; he was very dogmatic and dared Lilly to report him to the police. Of course she never reported him and was always very forgiving. Lilly became very accustomed to moving on with life as if nothing ever happened.

A few days after a violent episode, it was not uncommon for him to say that the incident never happened, nor did he have any recollection of it. It was unknown if Joe truly didn't remember or if he just wanted to separate himself from that magnitude of abuse. Nevertheless, he seemed to know just how to manipulate the selective amnesia. Lilly would often say, "He just lies his ass off." Of course she knew better than to say it directly to Joe for fear of opening another can of worms.

Joe regularly laid awake at night, ready and willing to pick a fight with Lilly. On several occasions, he yelled and slapped her around to the point where she tried to get away from him by sleeping in another bed, but he literally disassembled it so that she couldn't sleep in it. If she tried to escape by running into the girls' bedroom, which was right next door, he didn't hesitate to follow her in there and assault her right in front of them as well.

"I hated to go to bed at night because I knew that was his time to start a fight with Mama," said Carolyn.

"I wish he would just get it over with before we go to bed," said Denise.

"I never told Mama, but I never slept much either, because I knew daddy would find some reason to get mad and beat Mama," said Carolyn.

Both Carolyn and Denise's time in bed was usually spent hoping and praying that the night would soon end because at least they could get up and go to school and be away from the violence for a few hours. As children the girls witnessed too many violent episodes. To this day they both carry those emotional scars with them, and vow that they'll take those feelings to their grave. Like any other physical or emotional scar, they never forgot it, instead they just applied imaginary band aids to their emotional scars and just moved on. As a result of such undue stress, they often prayed for Joe to just pick up and leave the family and never return. Unlike him, when his father left, it greatly affected him, they honestly thought that they would have had no problem, or at least they wanted to see how it felt.

A typical episode went something very similar to this: On any given day usually at about 3:00-4:00 a.m., the whole house was very quiet, as they were all asleep except Joe. As they all slumbered and slept in the next room we were suddenly awakened by the loud noise of Joe's heavy voice. "Hey Lilly," Joe said. Next, there was a loud thump, which meant that he had shoved Lilly out of the bed onto the floor like a sack of potatoes, followed by the sound of screaming and yelling of all sorts of obscenities. The girls had no idea why he was so angry they just recalled Lilly trying to explain herself as if she was pleading in the hopes of reasoning and calming him down. Nothing she did or said seemed to make any difference. The more she tried to explain, the more the situation escalated, with him yelling even louder and louder, insisting that she had done or said something that greatly offended him. The next thing they knew he began to beat, push her to the floor, kick and slap her around. The horrible sound of such intense shuffling, along with bitter words of profanity and endless name calling remain forever etched in their minds.

As their hearts raced they clung to each other as they feared that their mother would die. "Oh dear God help us!" said Carolyn. In the next room, they could hear their mother crying and pleading for him to stop. Because of Lilly's size she was no match for him. She was less than five feet and he towered at least six feet, along with what seemed like the strength of ten men. Of course she tried to defend herself, but poor Lilly just lacked adequate strength. She always tried to flee from him but he always followed her while continuing to physically and verbally assault her.

The girls became frantic and began to cry and beg them both to stop. During his intense anger he wouldn't hesitate to turn the wrath on them by taking off his leather belt and beating them and telling them to shut up. He once said that if they ever tried to retaliate, he would get his gun and kill them all, and of course they believed him. Needless to say, they did as they were told, so poor Lilly would have to fend for herself as best she could. He left them feeling very nervous, confused and afraid, while he returned to Lilly who by then had left the upstairs bedroom and went downstairs to try to sleep on the couch. Although there were more threats of violence, he soon calmed down and returned to his bed.

After the violence took place, Lilly never said much, but Carolyn distinctly remembered her say on one occasion, "You gone suffa fo you leave here." He yelled back and said, "I don't care, I ain't got but one time to die." Lilly wanted him to know that he would someday reap what he sowed, which was her only defense.

As the morning grew near, Carolyn and Denise slowly and reluctantly got up and ready for school. Lilly was adamant that they keep the household incidents a secret and she assured them that she and everything at home would be all right. They were instructed to go to school and tell no one of the magnitude of violence that occurred, or they too were threatened by her with a beating if they shared the "family binness" according to Lilly. She said, "What goes on in this house, stays in this house."

Lilly was determined to carry on with life without letting others know that any of them had endured such violence. Although she often seemed very sad, she and Joe always seemed to carry on as usual until the next episode. This was the norm of the house, from the time the kids were old enough to remember until they left home for college. "Do you think our friends have to watch their mama and daddy fight?" said Carolyn.

"I don't know, but I hope not," said Denise. Of course, both of them knew better than to ask because they were too embarrassed, and also they were more afraid that news would get back to Lilly.

Now Joe and Lilly rarely went places together, but when they did there was never any indication of any violence. Conveniently Lilly's skin was dark and showed no sign of bruising so it made it a lot easier to disguise the physical violence. Of course, in the eyes of the community, they were quite the model family. They all carried on as if they were a happy and loving family. Amazingly, they were often complimented by members in the community for being such a nice family, which Lilly always graciously accepted. Lilly took great pride in keeping her house very clean and organized and also raising her children to be nice young ladies. "Learn to stay home and mine yo own binness," she said.

Joe didn't attend Church often, but when he did he was usually pretty irritated by the time he returned. He usually felt that the messages were specifically directed at him, or perhaps some of the members had intentionally ignored him because they didn't shake his hand. If Joe didn't like the sermon, he would abruptly stand up and march right down the center of the church and go back home. Typically his behavior caused quite a ruckus and since the old church pews were not nailed down to the floor, whenever he stood up, they rocked back and forth making a very loud distracting noise. The sound of his heavy footsteps also made a loud noise as well; and by that time, practically all the members of the congregation were no longer listening to the Pastor because they were now watching him make a complete fool of himself. Some of the members giggled at his childish behavior, and others just stared in total disgust. Obviously Joe would never be accused of being prudent.

"My heart sank because I knew he would somehow manipulate the situation and blame Mama for everything," said Carolyn.

Regardless, Lilly never let his behavior deter her from going to church because she was such a devout Christian and also this was practically her only opportunity, other than work, to be away from such a negative environment. She dearly loved to attend church because that was her special time to serve the Lord. Lilly loved and looked forward to Sunday mornings because this was her time to get involved in the praise and testimony service. No matter how bad things were at home she would stand up and testify, as if she were the luckiest woman on earth. Her favorite songs to lead were "This little light of mine, I'm gonna let it shine," and, "I don't know what I'd do without the Lord," as she swayed back and forth. She had no trouble taking the lead, nor did anyone else hesitate to join in with her. Lilly had such a strong dulcet southern tone which definitely set her voice apart from anyone else and by the time she finished, the whole church had done quite of bit of hand clappin and toe tappin to the sound of the music. Sometimes she would even stand up and do somewhat of a spiritual dance, which she could never replicate unless of course she became spirit filled again.

The girls loved to watch Lilly dance around the church, it was as if she had truly entered the presence of the Lord. Ah! What a glorious time she had in the Lord. Lilly also held a few positions in the church that boosted her self-esteem which made her feel important as well: Usher Board President, Youth Choir Director, etc.

Both of the girls were particularly proud of their mother for her church fundraising skills and activities. "I remember the time that she wanted the church to have an air conditioner, so she spearheaded several programs, held several bake sales, and even organized a fashion show to raise money," said Carolyn.

Although she had very little formal education, she went into town to speak to Henry, who was the owner of Henry's clothing store. Everybody knew that Henry's clothing store was upscale, but Lilly didn't hesitate to approach and invite Henry to be a part of her plan to help raise money for the church, which would also increase his business as well. Lilly cared less about Henry being wealthy and her being just a poor janitor who worked at the local hospital because her goal was simply to raise money for her church and she knew exactly how to run a successful program, but she needed support. Not only was Lilly personable but certainly very business minded as well. After listening carefully to Lilly's plan, Henry smiled from ear to ear and immediately agreed to support the endeavor. Lilly was absolutely ecstatic. She had exactly what she needed to organize her event and bring it to fruition. Now that the wheels had begun to turn, Lilly contacted several people that she knew in the community to act as models. She and quite a few of her friends prepared lots of good soul food and she even went to the local printing shop to have programs professionally designed and tickets printed, which she later assigned to some of the members to sell.

Needless to say the fashion show turned out to be quite the gala affair for many people of Albion. It was wonderful to see such a diverse audience, enjoying such a wonderful event, not to mention the soul food. It was even more special for the girls to know that their mother orchestrated the entire event. Without a doubt, the fashion show was a huge success and of course brought in lots of money for the purchase of the church air conditioner.

Afterwards, Henry mentioned to Lilly that some of the garments that the models wore were a bit soiled and could not be sold as they were. Lilly mixed no words and insisted that the items be professionally cleaned at her expense. She was determined to preserve the business relationship... "Binness is binness," said Lilly. When it was all said and done, Henry gave Lilly a beautiful pewter heart shaped necklace from his store, which really made her day. What a wonderful accomplishment for not only Lilly but for the church as well! Oh! By the way, "has anybody seen Joe?" said Lilly. Joe had somehow managed to stay out of sight for the entire affair. Although no one could account for his whereabouts, they all knew that he certainly missed out on a very festive occasion. Quite frankly nobody had time to worry about him at such an exciting time as this because everyone was too busy having an absolutely fabulous time.

On the other hand, Joe had quite a different experience when he attended church services. In spite of his very bitter and resentful remarks towards the members of the congregation, Lilly always tried to encourage him to ignore the members that he often referred to as "ol jealous asses." During praise and testimony service he would stand up to testify but his testimonials were most always filled with frustration, rage, and anger. He later told Lilly that he was very tempted to pick up one of the church pews and hurl it at the Assistant Pastor who he obviously despised. Of course she always tried to mollify and encourage him to ignore people. "Why don't you just pray about it," she said.

"Why don't you just kiss my ass," Joe replied.

"I think we would all be better off if we just stayed home and never went back to church," said Denise.

Lilly thought this was the most ridiculous thing that she had ever heard and further insisted that they attend Church as often as they could, which is exactly what they did at least four nights per week. Because of Lilly's sincere adulation for God, Carolyn and Denise eventually gave up on trying to persuade her to withdraw her membership in hopes of keeping peace at home because they just weren't getting through to her. Lilly genuinely felt that sacrificing the praise and worship of her Lord and Savior Jesus Christ was totally ludicrous, nor could she even begin to conceive of such an idea. "As long as I'm in my right mind I don't care what happen, I'm gone serve the Lawd," she said.

Carolyn and Denise said, "If hell freezes over Mama will be found at the Church singing songs, dancing in the spirit, and praising the Lord."

Since Lilly had no time for foolishness, she forged ahead with full force and gladly took the rebellious family to the house of God, after all … everyone always complimented her on having such a nice family and she always graciously accepted. Little did they know how specious the family really was.

There was one time in particular, when Joe went to church and testified that he had been called by God to preach the gospel. He assumed that he would be immediately assigned to a spot in the pulpit, as had been done so for many others in the past. Joe most often carried his Bible inside a briefcase, which made him look important and he really did look as though he could have been a Pastor because Lilly always made sure that he wore the nicest suits that she had either tailor made or bought from an upscale store.

Rather than the Pastor acknowledge him or at least try to explain his reasons for not allowing him to sit in the pulpit, he simply ignored him and overlooked his "calling." As time went on Joe became very bitter, embarrassed and downright angry. Needless to say, he stopped attending church at all. In all fairness to the Pastor, he was justified in his actions because he too was caught between a rock and a hard spot. Understandably, the Pastor could not afford to have Joe up in the pulpit spouting out insults to the members of the congregation because, based on Joe's past behavior, the pastor had no other information on which to make a decision. It was no secret that Joe had quite a temper and didn't mind telling the members of the congregation which way to go and where to step off. For certain, if Joe had been allowed to preach a sermon more than likely ninety percent of the congregation would have left the church out of sheer stress and fear. The other ten percent would probably stay long enough to see what would happen next. Obviously the Pastor was no fool and could read between the lines.

Chapter Four

Girls Fear Joe

Because Joe wasn't a very loving or kind father, neither of the girls were able to receive what they needed from him, so they learned at a very young age to lean on their mother for support. Joe was more of a figure that they feared. Although the girls were young, they figured out how to get along with him and stay out of his way. It was extremely difficult to know what was going to upset him, but if they did, all hell broke loose. They knew better than to question anything he said or did, even if they knew he was wrong. If Lilly wasn't home they asked him for very little. As a result, he would usually either refuse or very begrudgingly do what they asked.

Quite frankly they were downright afraid of him. If Lilly wasn't home or had to work late, they usually spent a lot of time upstairs in their room just sitting alone because they didn't feel comfortable being around him. They feared the tone of his voice, the heaviness of his rapid footsteps, the lack of patience, but mostly the verbal and physical violence that left them feeling helpless, hopeless, inadequate, and unworthy. On the other hand, Lilly was like a sweet and gentle butterfly swiftly flying around and going out of her way to placate him, but yet trying to boost the children's self-esteem, regardless of the fact that she too may have just been beaten or slapped around. Not only was Lilly beautiful inside, but certainly outside as well, which the girls felt was a golden gift from God. Lord only knows what life would have been like, had it not been for Lilly.

Although Carolyn and Denise thought their father was extremely curmudgeon, they constantly struggled to maintain a sense of normalcy. They didn't have many toys, so one day they both decided that it would be fun to jump up and down on the beds. After all they were just bored kids who wanted to have fun. Just as they were in the midst of having great fun, laughing at each other, all of a sudden a feeling of malaise came over them and they heard the sound of those heavy rapid footsteps rapidly approaching. Instantly they became real quiet as Joe rushed into the room screaming and cursing as loud as he could, snatched off his belt and began beating both of them with a belt that left big bloody welts on their legs. As they wept, they decided that they would never do that again. They learned another valuable lesson, just sit quiet and make the least amount of noise as possible because that's what he wanted.

The Sweet Potato Pie incident was another simply unforgettable story. First and foremost the rules of the house were "no food allowed in the bedrooms," under no circumstances; but because Carolyn dearly loved sweet potato pie, she wanted to have it in her room and enjoy it while she played with Denise. Like most children, she decided to sneak the pie upstairs when Joe wasn't looking. She sincerely had every intention of finishing it before he noticed, but regrettably she wasn't fast enough. In the midst of eating the pie, she heard those heavy rapid footsteps quickly marching up the stairs. Her heart began to race as she knew she would get in big trouble for having food in the bedroom, so she conveniently slid it just barely underneath the bed so that she could retrieve it later.

Joe rushed into the room and began yelling at the two of them for Lord knows what as he ordered Carolyn to "get out of the way." While trying to follow Joe's instructions her foot somehow got stuck in the pie and she went sliding across the floor as if she was a professional Olympic figure skater. What a sight! The Sweet Potato pie was smeared all over the floor and her slipper too. Although Joe was shocked and disgusted, he really didn't recognize what it was, nor did he ask! All of a sudden he stopped yelling about his original issue and began screaming at Carolyn to take her shoe off. Surprisingly she didn't get a whippin, he just yelled, "good God girl, take yo shoe off and clean that shit up" as he quickly marched back down the stairs just, as fast as he came up.

As he went back down the stairs, Carolyn looked at Denise who had the biggest grin on her face. "I really wanted to laugh at you, but I was so scared he would beat me but I can't believe you slid across the floor so fast," said Denise. By this time Denise had fallen to the floor laughing hysterically. "What a waste of a great piece of pie," Carolyn nervously said. "I was so scared, I could feel my hands sweating, my heart raced and I was sure I would get a whippin," said Carolyn. As the years went by the girls continued to find a lot of humor in this story, especially when they served Sweet Potato pie during the holidays. Fortunately the girls managed to savor at least part of the story, which has had no bearing on Carolyn's love for a good Sweet Potato pie. Yum! Yum!

Another crazy event that caused Joe's blood to boil involved Carolyn again. She was always doing stupid things, at least in the eyes of Denise. This time, she just happened to be wearing a dress with a long belt that was attached and tied in the back. Apparently Carolyn was bored because she untied the belt and began waving it over a small electrical hot plate that Lilly had placed in their bedroom to help keep them warm. After a few minutes the belt sparked a time or two and began to burn. A small flame slowly crept up the belt. "Oh my gosh, my dress is on fire!" said Carolyn. "I don't know what you did, but I'm gettin out of here," said Denise. "I'm scared, don't you leave me," said Carolyn. Denise immediately began running around the room trying to get away from Carolyn, who also ran behind her which only added oxygen to the fire. They were both frantic as they climbed up and down on top of the beds while running all around the room in circles screaming.

Once again they could hear the sound of those heavy rapid footsteps rapidly approaching. This time Carolyn cared less, because her dress was literally on fire. As always Joe busted into the room and began cursing like a sailor, but at least he put the fire out before he marched back down the stairs as quickly as he came up. "I'm so glad he put out the fire," said Denise. "Me too," said Carolyn as her belt continued to smoke. Fortunately Joe came on the scene before any serious damages occurred. It's really a pity that neither Carolyn nor Denise knew anything about the "stop, drop and roll" technique at that time because they might have gotten away with it. Of course when Lilly heard about the incident, she didn't say much and of course felt that the dress could be salvaged. After all, she didn't believe in wasting anything, as money was always scarce.

For some strange reason, Joe seemed to castigate Denise much more than Carolyn. There were times that he actually acted like he hated her. They could never determine his reasoning for doing so, other than the fact that she was the oldest and she resembled Lilly much more than Carolyn who resembled him, at least according to everyone else… Make no mistake, he didn't treat Carolyn like a Princess by any means but he really did seem to be downright nasty to Denise, for no reason at all. On occasion, she would bring friends home from school and it really seemed that he made a point of being even more nasty than he would have had she been alone.

Out of sheer embarrassment and frustration she finally stopped bringing anyone home at all because she was tired of his severe mood swings and angry outbursts, not to mention the comments that her friends would make at school the next day. On occasion, Carolyn would bring a friend home, and Joe's behavior was certainly nothing to brag about, but it was "almost decent" in her opinion. Denise was more outgoing than Carolyn, she was more interested in dating at a young age, and she really loved attending school dances, etc. Her mannerisms were very similar to that of her mother, which seemed to sometimes be very upsetting to him. On the other hand, Carolyn was more of a home body, very low key, low self-esteem, which he seemed to be a bit more tolerable of.

There was one particular incident when he demanded that the girls stop playing around and help him in the garden. While on the way to the garden, Denise made a very innocent mistake of saying that she did not want to help out, which really angered him; so he turned around and slapped her across the face as hard as he could. She didn't cry, but she was certainly stunned. Carolyn felt so bad because she knew that they were just young kids who wanted to play instead of do yard work.

Joe was in the process of recording one of his favorite songs. During that time Denise was either playing or talking, which he felt was too loud or not necessary and as usual, he became violently upset and yelled and blasted her. Of course this was very hurtful for her, especially because every time he played his taped recording you clearly hear him yelling and cursing at her in the background. At times Denise would ask Carolyn to take the blame for certain things so she wouldn't get in trouble with him, but Carolyn rarely did because she was just as afraid. Fortunately there was never any animosity between them. Like most siblings, they had their differences; but for the most part they always had a good relationship. Sadly, they both realized early on that their father showed favoritism, which had no place in the family as far as they or Lilly were concerned.

Chapter Five

Damn White Crackas

If Joe received a bill in the mail he automatically became upset with the mailman and made snide remarks. If his paycheck was short and he had trouble paying his bills, he would become extremely irritated with his creditors. The girls really felt sorry for any creditors that made the mistake of calling to remind him of past due accounts. He would cuss at them and call them all kinds of names and yell racial slurs. He referred to the bill collectors as those "damn white crackas," before abruptly hanging up. After hanging up, he would often say, "These damn white people is gonna do what they wanna do til Jesus come back."

Now Joe was no different from anyone else. He too was sometimes late paying his bills and of course his creditors would contact him via telephone, in hopes of at least finding out when they could expect to be paid. At one time in particular, one of his creditors called, but Joe was in the midst of taking a bath. Carolyn, who was an innocent bystander, made the mistake of informing him that someone wanted to speak to him. His attitude immediately changed and he became extremely angry. All of a sudden he stood straight up, got out of the bathtub and marched right over to the telephone. Not only was Carolyn shocked because he was dripping water and soap all over the place, but he stood naked and didn't even bother to put a towel around himself as he proceeded to yell and scream as loud as he possibly could. He obviously used every ounce of profanity that he could think of towards the poor old soul that was on the other end of the phone. After Joe exhausted his entire vocabulary, he slammed the phone on the hook and marched back to the bathtub, leaving a long and thick trail of soap suds all over the floor, as he proceeded to bathe himself and acted as if nothing ever happened. The entire incident happened very fast and occurred over a period of about two minutes.

Carolyn was totally flabbergasted as she must have been about ten or eleven years old at the time. "I didn't know whether to laugh or cry, but I knew better than to say anything because I was afraid that he would come after me too," said Carolyn. Of course Lilly wasn't home at the time; but it would have made no difference to him if she was, and she certainly would have known better than to try to remedy the situation. "I'm pretty sure that whoever was on the other end of the phone surely must have thought he was a total lunatic," said Denise.

Well, as time went on, the girls had reached high school age and Carolyn began dating a Caucasian boy by the name of Bob. Her biggest fear was that Joe would have a slip of the tongue and refer to Bob as a "white cracka," but fortunately he never did. Of course, she always knew when he was about to make a racial statement because he always very casually asked if Bob was present. Surprisingly, Joe really seemed to like Bob, which was a good thing because she eventually married him. Since the two of them began dating at the young age of fifteen, Joe wanted them to know that there would be no wedding until they reached the legal age of eighteen; and "I aint signing shit," he said. Although they had not planned and certainly didn't ask to wed before they were of legal age, he wanted it made known to everyone that he had no intentions of giving his blessings under any circumstances. Joe said he wasn't about to be blamed for anything, just in case things didn't work out.

Carolyn never heard Joe say one negative word about Bob during the entire six years of dating, nor did he ever give Carolyn one ounce of trouble about the wedding or anything else that pertained to Bob. All he wanted to know was what color suit he needed for the ceremony. "You betta tell me what color you want me to buy cause I'm only buyin one" he said. Now Lilly normally paid for his suits, but this time he actually insisted that he pay for his own. After the wedding ceremony, quite a few people of the congregation asked him how he felt about the marriage. Joe never hesitated and very loudly and bluntly said, "I don't have to live wit him, she da one that got to live wit him." Nobody in the congregation said another word after those remarks. Many years later, he frequently mentioned to Carolyn that he was glad she married him. Carolyn was always very proud of both her parents for the way in which they accepted Bob into the family. "There is good and bad in all races," said Lilly. "Amen to that," Carolyn said.

Chapter Six

Joe's Symptoms Become Unmanageable

Paranoia was another major piece of the puzzle. Joe rarely wanted to go to any restaurant unless it was the drive through. He said he didn't like it when people stared at him, nor did he prefer to sit too close to others. Neither Carolyn nor Denise could understand why he thought he was so special that anyone would actually want to sit and look at him, but then again they didn't have the nerve to ask! This was a real disappointment for the rest of the family because they seldom had the chance to eat out, especially since money was so scarce. As usual, Lilly never complained. Most of the time everyone stayed home and had dinner with him, but occasionally Lilly would take the girls to McDonalds, which they thought was a real treat. She always made sure that she left dinner on the stove for Joe to warm up at his convenience. If Joe ate dinner and all of a sudden didn't feel well, he later blamed Lilly by saying, "Woman I believe you dun put somethin in my food," even though we all would have just sat at the dinner table together and ate the same food. Although he never said, but the girls often wondered if Joe feared that Lilly would someday try to poison him as payback for all the abuse she endured.

He frequently accused and insisted that someone had been going through his bedroom closets and chest of drawers. Joe claimed that he left the clothing items stacked a certain way and he could tell if anything had been moved. Because Lilly insisted that the girls perform weekly chores that included folding and putting clean laundry away, it really wasn't too difficult to move some of the clothing items around from their original position. It was somewhat of a nuisance to try to make sure that nothing was disturbed especially when his laundry was clean, folded and ready to put away. At times he was adamant that the girls were lying and whipped them and if Lilly tried to say anything in their defense, she too would be beat. They all felt that they just couldn't catch a break!

Joe was very antisocial and very content just being alone. He didn't feel comfortable in crowded places. If he attended an event with lots of people, he would either turn right around and go back home, or he would definitely leave before the event concluded. The anti-socialism was so bad that he would make no effort to socialize with the neighbors that he had known and also despised for years. "I never ever heard one nice comment about any of our neighbors come out of his mouth," said Carolyn. "That's because he never did," said Denise. He always felt that they really didn't like him or that they were secretly plotting against him, no matter how friendly they appeared.

Late one night, he laid in bed stewing and complaining to Lilly about the neighbors. It seemed that the longer he stewed, the angrier and more frustrated he became. All of a sudden, he abruptly stood up like a flash of lightening, ran outside, jumped on his lawn mower and proceeded to ride up and down the property line for at least an hour. Between the big flashing lights and the loud noise of the tractor, in addition to the fact that he had a small radio that he turned up the volume to the highest level, it really sounded as if a Circus had come to town. Of course this occurred between 2:00-4:00 a.m., which was prime time for him. "I don't even remember what he was wearing or if he even took time to get dressed," said Lilly. "It's quite possible that he may have even worn his clothes to bed … who knows," said Denise. Now everyone knows that Superman is faster than the speed of light, but it was extremely doubtful that he could have held a candle to Joe. "I'm really surprised that nobody called the police to file a complaint for his disturbance of the peace and quiet," said Carolyn. Poor Joe, he was convinced that all of the neighbors hated him, but then again he was probably right, at least at that time

It was hard to believe that Joe was so antisocial and Lilly was so gregarious. It was really unbelievable to imagine that they were at one time attracted to each other. Clearly she was such a social bug, very outgoing and very comfortable meeting new people, whether in a large crowd or small group setting. Lilly was truly a people person. She loved to bake cakes and pies to give to neighbors and friends as gifts. She very much enjoyed looking through magazines, cutting out recipes that she intended to make with perhaps just a few modifications that would indeed earn her a seal of approval. Also it was very common for her to tell one of the girls to "take that Pound Cake across the street and give it to Mrs. Williams and don't drop it neither." Lilly had such a distinctive laugh, it was literally impossible to overlook her in a crowd, "ha ha ha hee hee hee, Lawd, I declare." It seemed that Joe resented the fact that she was so jovial and enjoyed being with people who actually seemed to like her as well. Although she genuinely tried to include Joe as much as she could, he just didn't seem to know how to mix and mingle, with people.

Chapter Seven

Feeling of Entitlement

Narcissistic behaviors also played a major role in his life. Joe's family may laugh now, but nobody laughed during his narcissistic episodes. Joe spent a vast amount of time talking about himself and all of his grandiose ideas of becoming wealthy. He often informed them of his intentions to buy any and everything that he wanted. Because Lilly wouldn't go along with him and support his beliefs, he vowed to divorce her as soon as he obtained all of his fame and fortune. This was pure foolishness according to Lilly who always said, "You got to put a dolla where you can see it." She would occasionally ask him to please put an offering in church, which usually never went over very well. He always said he would give the church money when, and only when he became wealthy.

For starters, he planned to build a mansion, purchase a Cadillac with a kit on it, buy houses for the girls and finally drive around so that everyone would look at him and be jealous. Furthermore, he claimed that he had a plan that would bring him wealth and it was all based upon the advice and information that was given to him by one of his so-called fortune tellers and or palm readers that he frequently consulted with for advice and sent money to. From one season to the next, Joe insisted that he would be wealthy following the next season. He never became discouraged and continuously insisted that his luck would change.

As he aged, the practice continued right along and nothing ever changed. Sadly this behavior and his obsession with money went on from the time the girls were small until his death. There was no way of knowing if he really believed that his luck would change, or if he desperately wanted everyone else to believe that his luck would actually change. He received infinite mail from all over the world promising to put his name into a Sweepstake drawing and or give him the winning number to become a millionaire. Both girls were often frustrated by the fact that he just didn't seem to understand that his name was only entered into a drawing, which meant that he had not actually won the Jack Pot. On numerous occasions, they tried to explain it to him; but he either wouldn't or couldn't understand. Sometimes Lilly would ask him why he thought anybody in their right mind would actually give him the winning numbers, rather than keep it and become a millionaire themselves. Joe never had any logical response, nor did he even try to understand the concept of what she said before he proceeded to send an additional fifty or one hundred dollars each time he was asked to do so by the Sweepstake Companies.

If Joe didn't have cash he wouldn't hesitate to use his Credit Card to obtain a Cash Advance to play the lottery. He always justified it by saying he would later reconcile with the creditors and pay all his bills from his winnings. Without any success, he even tried to control Lilly's money by telling her not to use her Credit Card without his approval because she needed to be able to provide for the family and handle any emergencies, at least until he was able to obtain his millions. Of course this didn't go over too well with Lilly who was very insulted and quickly informed him that her Credit Cards were for her convenience and not his. Also it was of no surprise that Lilly ended up closing their joint bank Checking account because Joe continuously wrote checks that bounced, which meant that Lilly was forced to pay the overdraft fees. Joe always refused to pay any fees and further claimed that he had indeed put money in the bank prior to writing the check, but obviously he did not. Since Lilly constantly struggled to pay the overdraft fees in attempt to remain in good standing with the bank; she soon grew tired, closed the account and they segued to using money orders. At least this way, they both knew they had to have money on hand in order to purchase a money order before they could pay their bills, which worked out pretty good for both of them.

Out of sheer desperation, Joe sought legal advice because he felt that one of the sweepstake companies had intentionally withheld his winnings. After the attorney listened carefully to his story, he told him to throw the mail in the trash, as it was all a waste of time and money. As time went on, Joe became very upset with his attorney and eventually had no further use for his services. Fortunately the attorney realized that Joe either had some mental issues and or was just plain ignorant and decided not to charge him for the visit.

If Lilly had a friend stop by for a visit, Joe most always managed to inform them of his intent to become a millionaire. Sometimes the guest would go along with him, but other times they would become very irritated and wondered if he was involved in a Ponzy scheme. Nevertheless, they never said a word to him as they could sense that he had problems along with a very short fuse, which was easily ignitable. Usually Lilly's guest would cut the visit short and leave looking very confused. Poor Lilly always tried to gloss over his ignorance and make excuses for him.

As adults, Carolyn and Denise always tried to be polite and invite him and Lilly over for dinner, especially to celebrate birthdays and holidays, but there again, he somehow managed to manipulate and ruin the occasion. It honestly seemed that Joe intentionally tried to control the conversation so that no one else could get a word in; and as a result everyone usually sat quiet and listened to him carry on about his presumptuous fantasy lottery winnings. It didn't matter that the grandchildren were home from college and wanted to share their experiences. It was as if he had no control and just wasn't happy unless he was the center of attention. If they tried to redirect him or change the subject, he became very upset and highly insulted. Because they were at their wits end, they finally decided to stop inviting him over for the holidays, which didn't make either of them feel good.

Of course, depression played a major role as well. Joe was definitely plagued with depression, but they never realized it. In hindsight, he really had nothing positive to look forward to. He didn't sleep well at night and he seemed to lay awake most nights fighting, yelling and complaining to Lilly. He had a job at the local factory that he was certainly less than thrilled with, but yet always went to work. He always insisted "I don't want no short check." Perhaps it was his obsession with money that kept him working because he had an awesome attendance record, even though he frequently complained about the coworkers, bosses, etc.

At the time, the girls were too young to understand all the details. However, they both remember he came home from work one day and told Lilly that he had gotten into an altercation with another coworker. Denise overheard him say that another employee had managed to get him on the ground while beating him. He didn't seem particularly concerned, but it was obvious from the looks of his face that he definitely didn't have the upper hand. His face was pretty bloody and scarred in spots. He said the next time someone took advantage of him, he would have to use his gun to shoot them.

Joe was practically illiterate and very resistant to take vacation time away from his job. Since he was unable to adapt to using new machinery and only knew how to run one or two machines, he didn't want to risk losing his spot when he returned. He once mentioned that he would fold the top of his time card in order to distinguish it because he had trouble reading his name. Unfortunately, there were others who would also bend their time cards because they had difficulty reading their names as well. The supervisor must have wondered why there were so many bent time cards in the slot, or perhaps they too knew that quite a few of their employees could not read. Somehow Joe always managed to punch in and out on the right bent time card. Lilly never remembered him being late or absent from work for any reason and he typically arrived at work at least thirty minutes ahead of time, as he said he wanted time to drink a cup of coffee and talk to a very select few of his coworkers before his shift began. He never deviated from this schedule.

The fact that there were very little to no vacations really didn't bother the girls at all because they typically went to visit elderly family members that they hadn't seen in quite a few years. There were actually very few relatives within their age group, so they really didn't have much to be excited about. Their other problem was that Lilly always required them to do quite a bit of heavy duty house cleaning upon their arrival. To no surprise, Lilly had very high standards when it came to cleanliness. She always insisted on having everything cleaned and sanitized before she would give her verbal consent to unpack the suitcases. Whenever the girls complained she simply explained, "I just can't sit in nobody's filth."

Needless to say it didn't take long for the girls to realize that their "vacation" wasn't really going to be a fun filled vacation after all. On the flip side, the relative of the home they visited was utterly delighted when they arrived and always very sad to see them leave. Not only did Lilly insist on having a clean house, but she wanted everyone else to make a habit out of being clean individuals in general, freshly bathed, and to uphold a tidy appearance as well. If either of the girls had a continuous itch on any part of their body, she assumed that they were dirty and recommended that they take a bath. "Girl go get yo self in a tub of hot watta or at least as hot as you can stan it," which was Lilly's solution to just about everything including skin problems, arthritis, and headaches before going to the doctor.

Chapter Eight

Joe Hears Voices

Eventually Joe began to exhibit signs of Schizoaffective symptoms as well. Lilly and the girls was amazed at some of the things he claimed that the voices or "them people" were telling him. He often said, "Them people told me you was workin gainst me." He would often say these words to Lilly, but he could never tell her exactly "what people" he was referring to, even if she asked. He knew that she prayed and read her Bible daily, which really seemed to irritate him. Although she wasn't the best reader, she did pretty well. She was determined to read her Bible for herself and not take any preacher's word. If Joe happened to see her reading her Bible he would become upset and insist that her prayers would somehow jeopardize him winning the lottery. Little did he know that telling Lilly not to read her Bible was like saying to the sun, "Don't shine."

Come hell or high water, Lilly was determined to read her Bible and serve her Lord and Savior, her Prince of Peace, and her Mighty King, no matter what. The more he insisted that, "them people," were telling him that she was the cause for his bad luck, the more she would delve into the scriptures of the Bible. It was absolutely comical! The girls honestly felt that Lilly must have been born with a Bible in one hand and a cleaning cloth in the other. Of course, Lilly would sometimes ask him, "Do those people ever tell you to be nice to yo wife?" But of course he never responded. Neither Lilly nor the girls ever believed Joe, or much less that, "those people," ever existed.

The front lawn had three Yew shrubs that were growing nicely in front of the house. The bushes should have actually grown about four feet tall and would have really enhanced the front porch. However, he refused to let them grow beyond two feet and insisted that people were hiding behind them. Lilly never acknowledged his remark nor did she ever question him about cutting the bushes so short. She decided that this was one battle that just wasn't worth fighting.

Joe also had an issue with the girls walking on certain areas of the lawn. This was rather difficult because the house sat on approximately two acres and the girls loved to run all over and enjoy the property. He claimed that he could tell if "those people" had contaminated a specific area that had caused him bodily harm. He insisted that he could sense the contamination, based on the amount of pain he felt in his joints. Lilly suggested to Joe that perhaps he just had arthritis and should see the doctor, but instead he vehemently disagreed.

Joe had a horrible gambling addiction that continuously spiraled out of control. As time went on, he managed to completely relinquish and nonchalantly pass his share of the bills to Lilly, and insisted that he had no other options; after all, he felt that he was looking out for the best interest of the family. Because he was quite the spendthrift, he demanded that Lilly pay all the bills. Of course she rebelled as she was a little spit fire when it came to somebody taking her "lil taste of money." "You just gone have to kill me cause ain't nobody gone take my lil money way from me," she said, which sometimes Joe vowed to do just that.

By this time. Joe was corresponding with what seemed like every sweepstake company in the nation. The mailbox was always stuffed full of letters from companies asking for money in order for him to be put into the million dollar sweepstake drawings. Each letter was like dangling a carrot in front of a horse, which fascinated him to no end. He surely loved it when the mail came and acted somewhat like a child at Christmas time. Needless to say, he wanted to be the only one to retrieve the mail from the mailbox. If anyone else went towards the mailbox he immediately said, "naw, naw, I get it." After he retrieved the letters from the box he always sat quietly by himself studying every sentence of the literature, trying to decipher just how wealthy he would become after paying his entry fee.

Sometimes he had quite a gale of laughter as he anticipated that he would soon be filthy rich. At that particular time he had a charge card, which he used continuously to obtain cash advances. It never occurred to him that he would one day have to repay this money, and of course stood firm that he wasn't worried because he would have no difficulty paying it back once he became a multi-millionaire, perhaps even a billionaire according to his fortune tellers. He made it quite clear that Lilly was not to badger him about it or anything else for that matter, until that time came.

Lilly continued to insist that she had a bad feeling about his plan and she adamantly warned, "You aint neva gone see daylight if you don't start savin yo money and use wisdom." "Every time you give them sweepstake people a lil piece of yo money they aint neva satisfied and want you to hurry back to give em some mo of yo money," she said. Lilly knew in her heart that Joe would never be debt free at, least on this side of heaven which apparently was the least of his worries. Once again, Lilly's predictions held true. After several years of gambling and receiving no return, the creditors came after him like a hound dog in search of a fresh kill. The creditors were vicious and demanded that he make the necessary arrangements to pay his bills immediately. Since he constantly received numerous phone calls that rang off the hook and threatening letters; he finally stopped answering the phone. If anyone else answered the phone, they were told to hang up or lie and say that he wasn't home.

Nonetheless the family survived because Lilly was very assiduous, extremely frugal, not to mention an excellent seamstress. When she shopped, she bought everything on sale: food, fabric, etc. When Carolyn got her first job at the age of sixteen, Lilly no longer bought her clothes. She instructed Carolyn, " Always shop at them nicer stores and go straight to the clearance rack so you can get somethin good without payin a whole lot of money; but if you aint got no money, then just stay home and don't be doin no window shoppin neither," said Lilly. Also Lilly just didn't believe in buying oversized clothes, she said, "don't neva buy yo clothes too big, you always work to stay in them small sizes." "And one mo thang…don't give nobody no cheap presents they can't use for Christmas or a birthday present, and if you ain't got but two or three dollas, just give 'em the money so they can at least put a little gas in they car," Lilly said.

As soon as the girls were old enough to work, Lilly required both of the girls save enough money to pay for their own life insurance because "that's one bill you don't neva want to leave for nobody else to take care of," she said. On the other hand, Joe wanted no part of any life insurance policy or anything else, but Lilly said, "You ain't gone lay up here and die on me and have everybody lookin' at me." Lilly had no intentions of being the topic of discussion at the church. Nonetheless, Joe cared nothing at all about anything she said and insisted, "I ain't leavin' you nothin' to spen when I'm gone." Joe figured he would continue right along with his gambling habit and, in the case of his death, Lilly could use those funds. "Ain't no undataka gone hold yo body while yo property being sold, you fool," she said. Lilly, being the gorgeous butterfly that she was, gladly paid his monthly life insurance bill and she had every intention of providing him with a decent burial, especially if she was the last survivor. "I ain't got no lot of education, but I don't want nobody thinkin' I'm a fool cause I ain't got no money to bury you." At that time the insurance agents made house calls to collect the money, which Lilly always planned for. Neither of the girls ever forgot Lilly's words of wisdom.

Chapter Nine

Head Piece

Because of Lilly's integrity and friendly personality, she was even allowed to open a credit account at the local Goodwill. She made sure that the girls had what they needed, especially the basic necessities plus one or two extra niceties. All in all, she carried the load. "You got to learn how to paddle yo own canoe, don't neva depend on no man to take care of you and always make sho you pay fo yo head piece befo you buy anythang else no matta what," Lilly said. Lilly was always very concerned about the house payment, which she referred to as the "head piece."

She wasn't about to be homeless with her family even if she did have to carry the load. Any other bill was always secondary to the "head piece." Lilly was no fool and knew she couldn't depend on Joe, but yet she wanted to hold the family together and she had no trouble taking the lead. She even tried to help him make a little extra money by talking a few of her friends into letting him mow their grass, which he actually seemed to enjoy most of the time. Joe was extremely parsimonious and never gave Lilly any more than twenty-five dollars per week for groceries.

Surprisingly, the amount of money he gave her never changed from the time the girls were small, until the time they left home. He either didn't realize or perhaps he just didn't care that growing children could easily eat more than twenty-five dollars' worth of food per week. Had it not been for the garden that they planted, everyone would have starved. Lilly told the girls not to worry because she could always make "pannigravy," if she had too. "What is pannigravy, Mama," said Carolyn. "It ain't nothin but a lil flour, grease and a lil watta that my Mama use to make when I was a lil girl. You put it on top of rice or sop it up with a piece of toast," said Lilly. Although he didn't believe in spending very much on groceries, he always made sure that he kept his old truck running so that either he or Lilly could provide the girls with transportation to and from school, especially during inclement weather.

Although witchcraft isn't a mental illness, it goes right along with all the other dysfunctional behaviors that contributed to Joe's demise. It was quite common for the girls to come home from school and find Joe sitting in a corner all huddled over two or three good luck charms, burning candles and reading books or Tarot cards on how to put spells on people. Sometimes he would brag to Lilly that he had the power to make women love him, obtain wealth, and even "fuck people up" if they messed with him. He claimed that he could cast magic spells or use specific lotions and potions to accomplish his goals as well. Sometimes he even threatened to run Lilly crazy too. "I can order as much shit as I want to," said Joe.

Of course, Lilly didn't support that type of behavior and said, "It aint nothin but a trick of ole Satan," who she adamantly described as "the enemy." Lilly always made clear to the girls that this was one of the main reasons she wanted to leave the South. In addition to there being too many large poisonous snakes that she was afraid of, she insisted that the South was "full of palm readers, fortune tellers, and witchcraft." She cautioned the girls about witchcraft and sternly warned them about leaving any strands of their hair in the trash can for fear that someone may use it to mix up some concoction, which could "run you crazy." Under no circumstances did Lilly plan to take part in it, nor did she want her children brought up believing in anybody other than God.

On the other hand Joe clearly indicated that regardless of what Lilly said, there were definitely some positive life changing benefits that could only come from witchcraft and palm readers. Joe swore that these people had been given special gifts from God that would enable them to divulge the winning lottery numbers for starters. If he wanted a reading and didn't have money to pay, he would simply bargain with the Fortune Tellers or Palm Readers by bringing stamps, cans of coffee, or whatever he thought he could spare from home, according to Lilly. It was really rather comical to think that anyone would agree to be paid with stamps or coffee, instead of money. It just goes to show that one should consider the source, which clearly Joe never did.

Regardless of the fact that he was in a state of financial ruin, he remained in denial and insisted more than ever that the fortune tellers and palm readers had promised him that he would one day be a wealthy man. Joe hung on to those words as if it were his lifeline. It was really such a pity that he couldn't see that it was Lilly who was indeed his lifeline. He just couldn't get past the fact that maybe, just maybe, he had been lied to. "I might be dead and gone sleepin in my grave but one of dees ole days he gone see where them folks was just lyin to him," said Lilly.

Poor Lilly, she constantly pleaded and tried to reason with him about the fortune tellers and palm readers. She passionately insisted that they were doing nothing more than making a complete fool of him. Lilly just couldn't understand and often said, "He let everybody make a fool of him but me." Even though he ignored her she continuously tried to help by insisting, "You got to put yo money where you can see it." Spending money without getting something in return was absurd, as far as Lilly was concerned. "I'm sho glad God give me a lil bit of wisdom," she said. Lilly always needed to see exactly where her money was going or she just wouldn't part with it under any circumstances.

There is certainly no sense in leaving out pornography since Joe dabbled in that area as well. Both Carolyn and Denise noticed that he sometimes spent quite a bit of time alone in the basement. There was nothing exciting about the basement, other than the fact that Lilly's sewing shop was there and also a washer and dryer that was in another section of the basement. Directly across from that was a very tiny closet positioned directly underneath the stairway where Joe kept his dirty work clothes and boots, which he said he preferred to keep away from the regular laundry because they were extremely grungy as a result of the factory where he worked. Other than a few cobwebs that needed to be knocked down, there was really no reason to go to the basement or the closet.

Nevertheless, the girls could never understand why he became so angry with them whenever they went in the basement, especially if he was already there. Every Saturday was chore day, at least as far as Lilly was concerned; and everything always got a good cleaning, whether it needed it or not. Lilly routinely sent the girls to the basement to fold laundry or to iron clothing. There was one time in particular that they were both bored and started fooling around, just laughing and talking. Leave it to curious Carolyn who just happened to wander over by the tiny closet and open it for no other reason than just to take a closer look. They both laughed hysterically at the discovery of a pile of about six adult magazines and an old movie projector that Joe used to watch pornographic movies. "Well, now we know why he never wanted us down here when he was here," said Denise. Of course they were pretty embarrassed, but knew better than to mention their discovery to Lilly or Joe, as they knew they would become very angry. At this point, nothing surprised them.

Chapter Ten

Where Is The Love?

Quite frankly, neither of the girls ever heard Joe verbalize that he loved Lilly, nor did he ever make any kind of romantic gestures. They often wondered why they never saw him give Lilly hugs or kisses, but they do recall Lilly occasionally attempting to give him a hug, which he never welcomed. Joe would always push her away or act as if it was a real bother to him. For many years the girls wondered if they were their legitimate children and if so, *what were the circumstances in which it occurred?* There again, neither of them had the nerve to ask. On one occasion the girls specifically recalled the two of them having an argument, which was nothing new; but this time it involved a woman who lived just around the corner and had her lawn mowed by Joe.

Lilly said, "I aint gone stay wit you runnin." She made it quite clear that she would tolerate no extra marital affairs, although she currently put up with more than her share of abuse. "A saw cut goin and a saw cut comin and if a man is married to a good woman then he sho betta have sense enough to keep her and if a woman marry herself a good man, then she betta have sense enough to keep him too," Lilly said.

Joe never had anything logical to say other than the fact that he intended to mow the woman's grass whenever he pleased. "If you like that woman, then you just easy to please cause she don't look like nuttin to me," she said. According to Lilly, Joe was obviously just "hot in the tail." Lilly was adamant and insisted to the girls that they should, "Neva mess wit nobody's husband cause you aint gone do nottin but mess yo life up foolin wit a dog gone man and don't let him wink his eyes at you neither. Tell him to go on bout his binness and whatever you do don't be beddin up wit no man neither," Lilly said. She definitely did not support the idea of living together, regardless of the reason. In her opinion, the individuals were just shacking up, which was a sin. "Now you go on and get yoself married even if it don't work out, at least give it a try," she said. "Now did y'all undastand what I dun tol you?" Lilly said.

"Yes Mama," they both knew that they better respond correctly or she may whip them too. Lilly didn't care if the girls were of legal age, she would have knocked down their door and dragged them away from whomever they happened to be shacking up with. After all, Lilly was a very devout Christian, and she strongly felt that the girls should behave in the same manner.

Well, as time went on the marriage continued to spiral out of control. Each day was like watching a tornado pick up speed and create irreparable damage. Joe continued to speak to Lilly in a very condescending manner and was adamant that he no longer wanted to eat her cooking nor sleep in the same bed. By that time he made it clear to her that he intended to contribute nothing more towards the household bills. He seemed to be full of excuses as to why he couldn't help out with the cost of any of the utilities each month and he often dared her to complain. He frequently said he hated her and vowed to get rid of her in one way or another. She was damned if she did and damned if she didn't. He resented her asking him any questions about anything. She couldn't even ask if there was any mail without him assuming that she somehow intentionally insulted him.

One afternoon in particular, Lilly made a completely innocent comment or asked him a question and he became so violent that he picked up a wooden dining room chair and struck her in the face with it. Her whole forehead swelled, which looked something like that of a unicorn. Of course she cried as a result of the pain, but she said or did nothing. Lilly and the girls stood in a frozen state. Later she noticed that one of her front teeth was cracked as well. They were all in shock, as there was no warning that he was upset. Joe literally went from being very relaxed and calm to extremely vicious and vile within a matter of seconds as he stood there cursing and screaming that he would kill her if she didn't shut up.

Again she chose not to seek medical attention and insisted that everything be kept secret because the girls should never disclose her personal business. Lilly sadly said, "Lot of women have it much worse than I do and as long as he don't get his gun or knife after me, I think I be o.k." Joe was basically a human landmine in the eyes of his family.

The girls were literally afraid of him and even more afraid to disagree with anything he said or did. As the physical and verbal violence continued to escalate he became even more out of control. "I was so scared, I honestly thought he was gonna kill Mama," said Denise.

Joe's driving was no different from the rest of his life. He was a rude highway driver. It was as if he took great pleasure in driving a mere inch from the car in front of him. He would yell and curse at the cars to get out of his way, and then he would swerve around them going at least 100 miles per hour. If Lilly and the girls happened to be in the car, it made no difference to him. Lilly would plead and beg Joe to slow down. "Oh honey please slow down, you gone kill all of us," she said. Joe ignored her and drove without stopping. "Oh Lawd, protect us and shield us from all hurt, harm, and danger," Lilly said. Carolyn and Denise sat quietly in the back seat, hoping that Joe knew what he was doing. Lilly always said she would never ride with him again, but as usual she always accompanied him. Fortunately Joe was never involved in an auto accident as there were no seat belt laws at the time. Perhaps the good Lord heard Lilly's prayers and watched over them.

Another incident involved the family dog that the girls really loved. They had a very young German Shepard that seemed to constantly bark, which is certainly not unusual. For some strange reason, Joe never wanted the dog to be out of its pen nor did he want to hear the dog bark. There were many times the dog wouldn't stop barking, which angered Joe to no end. He wouldn't hesitate to take off his belt, go into the pen, pull the dog out of its house and beat it until it yelped and yelped and yelped. The kids felt so sorry for that dog because Joe made it spend its whole life outside in the pen, which most likely contributed to the development of arthritis in the hind legs that eventually warranted euthanasia. Of course the girls were sad but also glad when the poor dog finally died.

Since the girls had never owned a bicycle, Lilly thought it would be nice to buy them each a brand new 10 speed bicycle, which they only had for approximately one week. One day while riding, Denise's chain came off and she made the mistake of asking Joe to help her put it back on. After a couple of tries with no success he became extremely irritated and angry, which resulted in him picking up the bike and throwing it across the yard, completely ruining the frame. Needless to say she was unable to ride it and of course she dared not say a word to him because she knew it would turn into something ugly for everyone. Joe never mentioned repairing the bicycle and just went on with life, just as he had done so in the past. Fortunately, Carolyn was nice enough to share her bike, but it was really rather awkward because they could no longer go for rides together.

Years later the girls were very excited about having Lilly's mother, Grandma Elnora and Joe's mother, Grandma Emma come for a visit, as they both wanted to attend Denise's wedding. Both Emma and Elnora were also pretty excited about the visit, as neither of them had ever spent time with the family. Of course everyone was excited to have company for such a festive occasion. Now Joe seemed fine, at least for the first couple of nights; but after that his true colors came out loud and clear. By the end of the week, Grandma Elnora was in tears and he ordered her out of the house, after accusing her of all sorts of things that were simply untrue.

Lilly was very hurt and embarrassed as she had to arrange to have another relative take her mother elsewhere, not to mention explain why her mother couldn't stay with her, while Joe's mother was made to feel very welcome. Fortunately Elnora was able to attend the wedding, but Lilly had to make sure that she was never anywhere near Joe. Once again, Lilly chose to keep peace in the family and enjoy the wedding that she had worked so hard to arrange. Afterwards, she never said one word to Joe about her thoughts or feelings.

Towards the end of the marriage Lilly endured a broken arm as a result of one of his violent outbursts. As always she was reluctant to contact the police. After all, she had never done so before. Following the incident she went to bed and hoped to feel better the next morning, but instead she felt worse. The next day she mentioned to Joe that she thought her arm was broken; and like always, he showed no remorse and said, "I don't care, at least I ain't killed you."

Because she could no longer tolerate the pain, she had no choice but to go to the hospital and report the incident. Lilly felt very emotionally drained, embarrassed, humiliated and ashamed of herself for having put up with him for at least thirty-five years. There she sat, surrounded by many coworkers that she had known and worked with for many years. Everyone was shocked as they assumed that this was the first occurrence. Little did they know, this was the result of a lifetime of violence. Lilly wondered if they really didn't know… or perhaps had just been too polite to comment. Naturally, everyone wanted to know if she planned to seek legal protection and file for divorce. It was no surprise that she was very reluctant and definitely didn't want to go down that road.

By this stage neither Carolyn nor Denise lived at home, but of course they were well aware of the ongoing domestic violence that Lilly chose to endure. After the hospital visit, she notified both the girls of the incident as she needed emotional support. They were both in tears when they learned of the violence that resulted in Lilly's arm being broken. "I want you to go straight to the police and file for a divorce," said Carolyn.

"No I can't," she responded. "Why not?" said Carolyn. "I don't know if I can take care of myself," said Lilly. "What do you mean Mama, you've been paying all the bills by yourself for years and Denise and I don't even live at home anymore," said Carolyn. "Either you report him to the police or stop telling me about any more abuse because it hurts me too much to hear about it," said Carolyn. "Okay, okay, okay," said Lilly.

Chapter Eleven

Lilly Breaks the Silence

For the first time in her life Lilly couldn't hide the abuse. She had always been able to hide the fact that she had been slapped, shoved, or called ungodly names but she couldn't hide a broken bone. Poor Lilly, she had what seemed like the weight of the world on her shoulders. She had spent her whole life hanging on to God with her right hand while struggling to hang on to her family with her left hand. She was absolutely emotionally exhausted. Even though she had a very abusive husband that she loved, she knew that she couldn't continue down the same path. By this time she had two adult daughters who demanded that she leave Joe, along with several coworkers that she had worked with for many years who also pressured her to seek legal advice.

Because Joe showed no remorse, which the girls felt he never did, Lilly feared that the abuse had escalated to another level, and she reluctantly agreed to have Carolyn pick her up and drive her to the police station. Although she was hesitant, she did file a report with the local police who informed her that he would be picked up for questioning. Well, Lilly waited one week, which turned into two weeks and finally three weeks and still nothing happened. She finally called the police station to ask the officer if he had any specific information as to when Joe would be picked up. After all, she and Joe were still living under the same roof and his attitude had not changed.

She was given no information, other than "soon." Perhaps the delay may have had something to do with the fact that her report was extremely atypical, at least in Carolyn's opinion. Carolyn complained that Lilly's report was directed more towards Joe's medical conditions and much less focused on the fact that she was the victim that sustained a broken arm, as a result of the abuse. Carolyn went on to say that never in her life had she heard of a victim providing so much extensive medical information regarding the fact that Joe was a diabetic and would need to have plenty of fruits and juices on hand to eat and drink, just in case he had to spend time in jail.

"I don't know whether to laugh or cry," said Carolyn. Fortunately for Joe, he was never picked up, but instead was told to meet at the court house within thirty minutes of the trial. When he arrived, the Judge sternly informed him that he needed to move out if he couldn't get along with Lilly. Of course no jail time occurred, most likely because nobody wanted to be responsible for supplying him with adequate fruits or juices that Lilly claimed he would need! Following the trial, which only lasted about ten minutes, Joe came right home gathered most of his belongings and moved into one of their three rental properties that they owned. Before he left, he informed Lilly that he still wanted to keep in touch with her and be friends.

Now Denise thought his actions were ironic since he had previously vowed to get rid of her as soon as the opportunity had presented itself. Surprisingly, he acted as if he was concerned that he may never be able to see her again. Without hesitation Lilly agreed to maintain regular contact with him, as well and vowed to do whatever she could to help him with whatever he needed. Following the court ruling, they both continued to get together on a monthly basis to get groceries, pay bills and even stop at a restaurant for lunch. Since they both really loved fried fish, they typically went to Long John Silver's.

In spite of their situation, Lilly still truly loved him and said to the girls, "If anything ever happens to me he won't have sense enough to take care of his self." "Oh he'll be just fine, and stop worrying about him, why don't you worry about yourself for a change, after all you're the one with the broken arm," said Denise.

Chapter Twelve

Bizarre Behaviors

As time went on, Carolyn and Denise felt at least minimal obligation to maintain contact with their father and try to help him with whatever he needed; however, his mental illnesses definitely seemed to become even more pronounced after he moved out. It was no surprise that he hated his new neighbor and frequently accused him of breaking into his house, eating his food, leaving food crumbs all over the table, using dishes, living in his attic, and even using witchcraft on him. On several occasions he insisted that his neighbor was hiding in the attic and committing all sorts of heinous crimes.

Because his apartment was always in great disarray, both girls had a hard time believing his story because he was actually home ninety-nine percent of the day and they just couldn't imagine that anyone would have the opportunity to break into his apartment. Both of the girls felt that his thought processes seemed to be increasingly bizarre and there was definitely no chance of reasoning with him. Joe began making trips to the local police station on a regular basis claiming that his neighbors had stolen from him, but he never had any proof. Whenever he met with the police he was anything except calm; but, instead his mannerism was full of malice and rage. It was only a matter of time before the police figured out that it was actually he who had the problem and not his neighbor.

Because he made such a constant fool of himself it caused the police to monitor him even more closely, which definitely did not work in his favor. Out of desperation the police became very frustrated and often called Denise, to ask for advice and to suggest placement. Denise never made any attempt to do so, because she felt that no laws had actually been broken. Sure he made a fool of himself but he had caused no harm to himself or anyone else. Besides in her opinion, this was nothing new to her because he had always made an ass of himself.

Joe always received new clothes for his birthday and Christmas, but yet his physical appearance was similar to that of a bum, based on the fact that his clothes were always very dirty or torn. "For once in his life, I'd like to see him dressed in a nice pair of khaki's, a polo shirt and penny loafers, but I suppose that's never gonna happen," said Denise.

"Girl, now you know that ain't never gonna happen," Carolyn said. His socks always had big holes so that his toes either stuck out of the front or the heel was totally exposed. Joe's shoes were always untied and his breath was bad. Based on his offensive body odor, it was obvious that he desperately needed a bath. Neither of the girls ever paid much attention to him until he moved out because Lilly had always covered so well for him by letting him know when to change his clothes, bathe and even to brush his teeth if his breath was bad. He refused to pay for trash removal or barely any of his bills, for that matter.

He had a consolidation loan that Denise had worked really hard to get him, which should have helped him get out of debt; but unbeknownst to her he continued to mismanage his finances and once again managed to get behind on those payments as a result of gambling as well. Nobody was aware of the fact that he stopped paying his taxes and was also seriously in jeopardy of losing his houses, until he one day mentioned that he received a letter from the County, which indicated that he no longer owned the property.

While attempting to help with his finances, Denise discovered that he had been sent to collections for a past due bill, which she later determined that he was actually making at least minimal effort to pay the original creditor instead of the Collection Agency, which means that he was never given any credit for the few payments that he made. After spending quite a bit of time on the phone, she managed to obtain enough information to help Joe, at least direct the payments to the proper place in order for him to receive credit.

Joe refused to pay for heat and insisted on using a small kerosene heater to warm the one room in which he spent the bulk of his time during the winter. In order to prevent heat from escaping he covered the doorway with a sheet. It never occurred to Joe that he was in an enclosed room, inhaling toxic fumes, which subjected him to serious lung problems.

Out of sheer desperation to catch the neighbor in the act, Joe left the upstairs window open for the entire winter in attempt to freeze him out, meanwhile he sat huddled up in front of the kerosene heater in a tiny room covered by a sheet. Little did he know that by opening the window he exposed the old house to the elements and as a result completely ruined the walls and insulation. Needless to say his pipes froze and ruptured, which meant that he needed to hire someone to fix them. As usual, as soon as Lilly became aware of his dire situation her red flag went up and she immediately contacted a longtime friend, who just happened to be a handyman, to go and repair his pipes.

In the meantime, numerous people constantly phoned Lilly and Denise to enquire about the window being open on the house as everyone knew he resided there. As always, they tried to gloss over his ignorance by offering some type of meaningful explanation as to why Joe's windows were wide open during the dead of winter, but quite frankly there were no logical answers.

There was a horrible stench that came from the rotted half eaten food on the kitchen table and in the trash can that he claimed his neighbor had eaten and left. The inside of the refrigerator, along with the few food contents were all covered with mold. The kitchen sink was filled with water that obviously had not been drained in weeks perhaps even months, based on the odor. You literally had to hold your breath as you opened the kitchen window in attempt to get fresh air only to find that there was a lock that could only be opened from the outside! Meanwhile many gnats and fruit flies hovered throughout the house as if it was their natural habitat.

Joe had made absolutely no effort to clean or throw anything away. Although no one had ever witnessed seeing mice or roaches crawling around, it was assumed that they were present as it seemed like the perfect breeding ground. Quite frankly, both of the girls were terrified of mice and roaches and they cringed at the thought of having anything crawl on their skin. Fortunately Lilly had always kept the girls on a very strict cleaning regimen, so they never had to worry about any critters. Because Joe refused to pay for garbage service, he stored at least a year's worth of trash behind his house in an old trailer, which he had previously used for hauling his lawn mower.

Because he never took proper care of his dentures they literally disintegrated. Instead of storing his dentures in a bowl of water he chose to toss them in one of his chests of drawers. Joe just didn't have sense enough to realize that it was he that actually caused his dentures to become so very dry brittle. Joe didn't treat his dentures any better than he treated his real teeth. Because he never brushed his teeth he developed a serious gum disease, pyorrhea. Basically he had a mouth full of rotten teeth. He complained that the dentist extracted all his teeth and also scraped all of his gums without using any kind of numbing solution. Both the girls clearly remember him standing over the trash can while blood poured out of his mouth like a faucet. This went on for at least two days.

Chapter Thirteen

Destined To Be Homeless

Joe refused to pay the Auto Insurance on his truck, but yet he continued to drive it until the Police stopped him for a minor traffic violation and ordered him to park it. Eventually the tires went flat, and the Police arranged to have it towed away because they said that it was illegal to have it in his yard if he had no intentions of fixing it. He really didn't seem to be too bothered by it at the time, but later he said he planned to get it back one day. In the meantime, he walked wherever he wanted to go, regardless of the weather.

He stood out like a sore thumb because he always carried a crowbar for protection in one hand and a brief case in the other that contained all of his sweepstake literature that needed to be filled out by the girls who spent most of their time with Lilly. Once in a while the girls would be driving along and spot him walking; of course they never hesitated to stop and offer him a ride, which he always graciously accepted. Regrettably, by the time they reached his destination, the car wreaked as a result of his body odor. The girls felt sorry for him but never brought it to his attention, they simply rolled all the windows down and drove fast in hopes of clearing the air.

Joe finally informed Denise of the notification that was received from the City Health Inspector who had recently inspected the house with a fine tooth comb most likely at the request of the police and/or social services. Carolyn and Denise were told that the Health Inspector became physically ill during the inspection, which was most likely due to the foul odors and the insurmountable filth in the apartment. The poor guy probably had no choice but to seek medical attention for himself after such a horrid inspection.

Surely the Health Inspector must have wondered how in the world anyone could live under such deplorable conditions. At the conclusion of such an extensive list of citations, Joe was informed that he had only ten days to comply with the orders or the house would be condemned. Based on the girls' understanding of the citations, it would have been easier to bulldoze the house and start over rather than try to comply with any repairs that needed to be done because they estimated that the cost would have fallen in the range of seventy five-eighty thousand dollars, which was certainly unavailable to him. Joe was shocked and said, "I didn't know I could be told to get out of my own house, as long as I own the property."

As if that news wasn't bad enough, the girls found that Joe had also recently received a letter from the County that indicated his house was about to be seized because of past due taxes. Carolyn did her best to explain to Joe that the house was simply not fit to live in, based on the Health Inspector's criteria. Joe made the comment "I don't much care cause I don't want to live next door to that ole ass anyway." It was really a blessing that he took the news so well because the house was scheduled to be torn down shortly after the health inspector realized that Joe had no intentions of bringing the house up to code.

Now this was an extremely stressful time and quite a dilemma for Carolyn and Denise as they were perplexed as far as what they would do with their father, who was destined to be homeless without their help. Lord knows they didn't want him moving in with them, nor was it an option for him move back in with Lilly who was finally gaining some peace of mind. Once again Joe had managed to get himself in another predicament that he couldn't get out of. Carolyn and Denise knew that he definitely wasn't the easiest person to get along with, nor was he good about paying his bills; not to mention the fact that his credit was horrible, which eliminated almost all of his options. They actually thought of banning together and bailing him out of financial trouble, but quickly decided against it because of Joe's ongoing financially reckless behavior.

They began looking for apartments that were reasonably priced that he could afford and actually found several apartments that would have been perfect, but were unavailable to him as his credit was too bad. They even thought about having him rent one of Lilly's apartments, but they feared he would take advantage of her as he had often done in the past and refuse to pay his rent. In addition, her current tenants knew him very well and threatened to vacate the premises as soon as he moved in because of his personality.

Chapter Fourteen

Joe's Health Declines

Before any decisions could be made Joe fell and injured his back and was unable to walk. Fortunately for Joe, Denise just happened to drive by his apartment late one night and saw the light on and the door was wide open. She didn't see him walking around inside, so she stopped by to see if everything was all right. Surprisingly, she walked in there and found him lying on the floor. He was very weak but still conscious. He told her that he had fallen and hit his back on a chair and couldn't get up. Because of her Nursing background she realized the immediate need for medical treatment and called for the ambulance. Shortly thereafter, the ambulance arrived and of course Joe was very reluctant to go to the hospital, but he knew he had no choice because he couldn't stand independently.

For the first time in his life he felt helpless and dependent on others. By this time it appeared that he would need surgery. "I always knew that someday, something would slow him down, I just never knew what it would be," said Carolyn. Sometimes she would imagine that he would finally win the Jack Pot and suddenly be robbed of all his winnings, since he loved to boast and brag about his financial plans. But then again, she prayed that if he did actually win, he wouldn't be robbed or even killed as a result because he absolutely didn't know how to keep his mouth shut. Fortunately, neither of the two happened. "I guess the old saying is true… God watches out for fools and children and that includes everybody, at least to some extent," said Carolyn.

Following the surgery the doctors said he came through very well. They were told that the fall was caused by a blocked artery in the heart that required a stint. A day or two later, they noticed that he was still quite weak and unable to walk, nor did he have much strength in his hands. Denise questioned the doctors about his condition and was told that basically they were only concerned about his heart and he would soon be discharged from the hospital, regardless of all the other medical issues. The fact that he couldn't walk was attributed to his diabetes, which she knew was incorrect because he had been walking up until the day of the fall.

Because he was unable to walk and had previously lived alone, he was sent to a Skilled Nursing facility to receive Rehabilitative treatment. It was no surprise to find that he absolutely hated being confined to a nursing home. Ultimately his goal was to go back to his own home whether he could walk or not. On many occasions, he refused to participate in therapy and insisted that he would just "wiggle around in the bed" to accomplish the same goal. The Therapists became frustrated and finally stopped asking him to participate in therapy, which gave them more time to focus on other residents that actually wanted to improve their conditions. During his stay he was very uncooperative and at times downright belligerent with the staff and residents as well. If another resident became confused and entered his room he would cuss at them and physically shove them out.

One resident had to be sent to the hospital because Joe shoved him with such force that he hurt his arm according to the nurse. It seemed that he went out of his way to be uncooperative, but this was nothing new, at least to his family. Another nurse reported that she overheard him telling a deceased patient's family that the staff had killed him. Lord only knows what the family members thought after receiving this kind of news about their loved one, especially from another patient.

For some reason he didn't want to be touched by the nurses and he constantly refused to let them take his vital signs. Because Denise was a nurse they often had to rely on her to take Joe's vitals, as he was sometimes more tolerant of her, which was hard to believe. On one occasion he even took the foot rest off his wheelchair and threatened to hit one of the nurse's with it if she came near him. One of the nurses made the mistake of thinking she would perform a rectal examination on Joe after he complained several times that he was constipated, but Joe wasted no time letting her know and saying, "You ain't stickin nothin up my ass and get the hell out of here." Joe definitely hated everything about the nursing home. Because he couldn't leave the facility when he thought he should have, he became extremely angry, picked up a glass vase, threw it, and hit one of the nurses in the face as she sat doing her charting at the Nurse's Station.

Needless to say the Police were called to take him to the local Hospital Psych Ward. When he returned from the hospital he was given a single room as he continued to have confrontations with other nurses and patients. Carolyn and Denise thought the single room would make him happy since he always preferred to be alone; but as usual, he found fault with that too. As time went on, the staff became even more intimidated by him and as a result continued to call the Police to come to take him back to the Psych Department at the local hospital. Joe's abusive behavior towards the nurses went on for about a year or more.

Denise was told that Joe was evaluated, given several types of medications for depression, anxiety, anger, etc. which apparently had no effect based on his ongoing combative behaviors and severe mood swings. Once in a while the nurses would call the girls at home to try to get suggestions as to how to calm him down. They could clearly hear Joe yelling and cursing in the background ...."They aint nunna my damn boss, what the hell you callin them for." The girls would advise the nurses to hang up and immediately call the Police.

The entire process was like a revolving door and the poor nurses were emotionally exhausted and for the most part at his mercy. The girls were told that the Social Worker had contacted at least fifteen alternative facilities in hopes of discharging and placing him, but they all declined because of his combativeness. Understandably nobody wants to take on somebody else's problem. Both Carolyn and Denise were very disappointed because they assumed that all the trips to the Psych Ward would have proven to be beneficial, but not so. It was unclear why the Psych

Meds didn't seem to have any effect, perhaps he just needed mega doses. Sometimes he downright refused to take his medications and other times the girls were told that the medications seemed to have no effect.

Since Denise was a Nurse, Carolyn relied on her to ask appropriate medical questions and to follow up with the doctors. On the other hand Carolyn was a Social Worker and she took care of the financial issues that needed addressing as well. It was no surprise that Joe made it a point to bad mouth or sabotage anything Denise said or tried to do for him. He made sure that everybody knew, "She aint nunna my damn boss." Of course Joe had always been an expert at embarrassing the family in the presence of others as it seemed it was his specialty.

From the time the girls were kids Joe never cared about how they felt about anything. By this time they were all physically and emotionally drained. If they could have disowned him, they certainly would have. They too were sick of watching the nurses whisper and laugh at him, laugh at them, laugh at his stupid remarks and rude behavior. Quite frankly, had he not been related to them, they too would have laughed. They certainly didn't feel that he had been the greatest dad, and at this stage of the game they still had to try to somehow make sure that he received the proper care.

By this time Denise and Carolyn had reached a point where they no longer had the patience to deal with his BULLSHIT! By this time they both had their own families to attend to as well as look after Lilly whose health had also begun to decline. Because of Joe's irate behavior, they eventually decided to make fewer visits, which only seemed to escalate after they left. They really felt sorry for the nurses because they had to deal with him after their visits.

Nonetheless they forged ahead and did what Lilly taught them to do "just humble yo self, look over him and do what is right," she said. The girls were determined to get his health improved, get him physically walking, and have him back out on his own. They figured anything would be better than having to deal with him on these terms. Since Denise had many years of nursing experience and a great relationship with many of the hospital doctors, she approached them about Joe's medical issues to asked if they would take a closer look at him and perhaps ex ray his back in hopes of finding the cause of his problems.

She was informed that his spine was damaged as a result of the fall but could be corrected with surgery, according to the physician. Denise explained everything to Joe about the surgery, which he was very anxious and willing to undergo the procedure in hopes that he would walk again and "get the hell out of the nursing home," he said. Once again we were all in agreement for him to have the surgery. Indeed he had the surgery, everything went well according to the surgeon and surprisingly Joe even participated in the Physical Therapy.

As time went on his health and his ability to ambulate improved and of course he wanted to go home. Denise found him an apartment that she thought would meet his needs, but neither the doctors nor nursing home staff would agree to release him to live alone; as they felt he would need around the clock supervision. Denise came up with another plan, where she arranged to have a live in male that would be available to him in exchange for his living expenses; but Joe wanted no part of it and insisted that he would live alone, just as he had done in the past.

As an alternative Denise seriously thought about using his Social Security checks to make payments towards a small addition (one bedroom and a bathroom) to be added on to her house which he originally agreed to, but later profusely declined. Although Joe never said, they knew why he refused the offer. First and foremost he had a gambling addiction, which meant he wasn't about to give anybody his Social Security check to do anything other than play the lottery, and second, Denise really wasn't his favorite, so why move in with her? As a last ditch effort, the owner of an Assisted Living facility came in and asked Joe if he wanted to come and live at her home where he would have his own room and lots of unsupervised time during the day; but, as always he blew a gasket by providing the woman with quite a few choice words and sent her out of the building, just as fast or faster than she came in.

As usual Joe's intransigent stance prevented any progress from being made. Unfortunately they were back at square one. Carolyn and Denise were told by the physician that it would be an inappropriate discharge if he went home alone. Because both Carolyn and Denise worked full time, neither of them could make that commitment. Sure they could have told the doctor and nursing staff that we were going to provide around the clock staff and actually not follow through with it, but neither of them were going to lie because they knew full well that they couldn't be responsible for him to that extent, nor did they even want to spend that much time with him. By this time, Joe was furious and insisted that he wanted to go home, regardless of his circumstances, because there were others who were in a much worse shape than him.

Well, at this point it looked as if Joe would be a permanent resident at the nursing home. Of course he continued to blame and make everyone's life a living hell. His behavior issues continued to the point that the nursing administration asked us to remove him from their facility, as they felt they had done all they could do; and quite frankly they were tired of his abuse, phone calls to the Police, etc. Neither Carolyn nor Denise had any place to take him that he would agree to, so basically their hands were tied. At the time, he was his own Guardian and they legally had no authority over him. The nursing home held a legal hearing and the Judge spoke directly to him about his medical condition and his need for assistance. Joe informed the Judge that he had a sibling that lived out of State that would take care of him if he couldn't be alone.

The girls were told, at a later time, that the Judge had made contact with his sibling who verbalized an unwillingness to be responsible for his care. Next, the State Ombudsman arrived on the scene to review his case and attempt to remedy the situation. After no progress was made, the Nursing Administrator filed an application for the purpose of a State appointed Guardian since there was no Patient Advocate document in place. The girls were a bit perturbed because they didn't even know that this process was taking place but it really wouldn't have made any difference had they known, because Joe certainly wasn't cooperating with them; nor did either of them feel comfortable seeking Guardianship.

Within thirty days he was given a State appointed Guardian and was moved from one nursing home that he had been in for about two years, to another one that was much further away. Of course Carolyn and Denise felt really bad because the last thing they wanted for either of their parents was for them to end up being a Ward of the State. From then on, they had to drive twice as far to visit him, which was frustrating and greatly inconvenienced them since they both worked full time.

To make matters worse, Joe kept insisting that Denise was stealing money out of his account and consequently the State took control of Joe's bank account too. Denise's feeling were very hurt, not to mention the frustration she felt because she actually never touched any of his money, for any reason except to pay his bills at the nursing home. Denise felt that she no longer had any control over anything; but in retrospect she never had any control, she just thought she did. Later, Joe would ask them questions about his money and of course they would remind him that they had no way of knowing anything at all and he would have to ask his Guardian, which he claimed he hardly ever saw.

Although the new facility was not what anyone wanted, the girls felt that the nurses were very nice to Joe and tried to accommodate his needs. They also provided the family with a good report of his medical condition and behavior issues, which really shocked them. Some of the nurses even said they really liked him and that he actually had no behavior issues. He nonchalantly mentioned that the individual that transported him to the new facility literally dared him to cause any problems or his next stop would be jail. Joe said he wasn't sure who the person was that provided him with the information, but apparently he took him very seriously.

Although the girls were suspicious as to who the mysterious individual was, they were glad to finally learn that Joe had decided to behave himself. Perhaps the Guardian had a Police officer provide the transportation while giving him a stern talking to as well, which they thought was long overdue.

Nevertheless Joe just couldn't accept the fact that he was now a permanent resident of the nursing home and a Ward of the State. He continued to insist that he wanted his freedom and he continued to blame everyone else for not signing him out and finding him an apartment. "Y'all ought not to do me that way, and you oughta sign me outa here," he said. Of course they carried some of the guilt, but honestly they were plum tired of enduring a lifetime of verbal and physical abuse; not to mention the ongoing feeling of intimidation, especially since they were all grown up.

Basically Joe's family no longer wanted to deal with his explosive behaviors… after all he didn't hesitate to threaten to take his gun and kill them all; nor did they have any way of knowing what he was capable of doing, especially if he had been able to walk.

It took a while, but after taking a deep breath and a step back they realized that Joe's situation was not their fault or anyone else's. They didn't create his problem, nor did they have the miraculous powers to fix it. They did feel that he had been offered many alternatives, all of which he were declined. The fact that he chose to decline all offers was his choice alone. The fact that he wasn't able to cuss and bully his way out of the situation, as he had done in the past, was certainly not their fault either.

Lilly said, "Everybody's good thang runs out some time in life," He had finally run into a group of people that weren't going to be bullied, which was a good thing in their opinion. In retrospect, they all felt that Joe had actually been very blessed in that he lived to be as old as he was without ending up in prison or dead. So at the end of the day, Joe was miserable, which was no different from before. Through it all, Lilly always made sure that the girls took her to visit him as often as possible. No matter what happened that beautiful butterfly always came to the rescue.

Lilly always wanted him to know that she would visit him as often as she could get a ride since she no longer drove. As the months went on they all noticed that his health seemed to decline and he was moving a bit slower than usual. They weren't sure if his health was weakening and or if he was losing the will to fight, as he had done so all his life. Although they continuously made contact via telephone with the guardian and nursing home staff, it had been three months since their last actual visit, which they were not proud of.

Chapter Fifteen

Reflections

Since Joe's death they all had a lot of time to reflect on his life, which they feel was a truly a bittersweet experience. They did a lot of soul searching and were sure that Joe, too, had the opportunity to do some soul searching. Carolyn and Denise learned many valuable lessons from his death that they feel certain they would not have learned had he been alive. Carolyn said, "When God brings a person to mind don't put it off, go ahead and act on it either by way of a visit and or phone call."

As she thought back, she felt a strong sense of guilt because she actually had many opportunities to visit Joe in the nursing home, but she chose not to. God knew the day he would die and perhaps it was for her benefit, and her peace of mind to visit him before that time. "I can't be sure but maybe dad wanted to share something with me or just spend time with me before he died," she said. "Don't hold a grudge against nobody for what they do, cause it aint nothin but a waste of time and sides that, God said he would be da judge," Lilly said.

"I feel like I wasted a lot of precious time being mad at him for acting the way he did, when really the personality and mental disorders had such a strong hold on him that he wasn't capable of making good decisions," said Carolyn. "There were many occasions when I could have spent more time with him, but I chose not to do so because I was very angry and I intended to prove it to him by ignoring him," replied Denise. "He embarrassed me so much until I had a hard time claiming him as my father." Joe must have at least realized that he hardly received visits from family members because he would ask "when you comin' back?" They never gave him a specific response.

When individuals are plagued with severe mental illnesses, without a doubt they are not only extremely difficult to manage, but also rather impossible to live. It's very difficult to look beyond severe verbal and physical abuse and see the illness as being a separate entity. Amazingly Lilly was somehow able to look beyond the mental illness to see that Joe needed her love and patience. "How in the world can we get round not forgivin' somebody else when we steady askin' God to forgive us?" which was Lilly's rationale.

Now Lilly never understood the science behind the mental illness, she just knew for sure that, "Honey was just a hard person to live with," she said. Fortunately for him, she saw the bigger picture. There's a scripture in the Bible that reminds the girls of Lilly, which comes from 1 Corinthians 12:4-7 and reads: "Love is patient, love is kind. It does not envy, it does not boast, it is not proud. It is not rude, it is not self-seeking, it is not easily angered, and it keeps no record of wrongs. Love does not delight in evil, but rejoices with the truth. It always protects, always trusts, always perseveres."

Although he often verbally and physically abused her, Lilly never stopped loving him and she stayed married to him as long as she possibly could. She strongly believed that she should hold the family together. Based on her upbringing, a woman never left her spouse, regardless of the home situation. Yes, she could have retaliated and physically hurt him and ended up in prison; and Lord only knows what would have happened to the girls. On the other hand by remaining in such a volatile relationship she exposed herself and the girls to a lifetime of violence that they should have never witnessed.

Nevertheless she made the decision to try to make the marriage work, but when she realized that being married was no longer an option because Joe had so recklessly spun out of control; she very reluctantly divorced him after thirty-five years of marriage. In spite of the abuse and the divorce, she remained a genuine and loyal friend.

She also continued to pay for his Life Insurance. Many times the girls discouraged her from keeping his insurance policy paid up to date, but she insisted that she would do so as long as she lived. She even encouraged the girls to carry their own life insurance policies on her to ensure that they would have adequate funding when she died. Lilly wasn't the least bit worried about the girls becoming greedy and using the insurance policies as a reason to hasten her death. Lilly felt that she could trust her girls and they dearly loved her as well.

When Joe died not only did Lilly use the funds from the policy to pay for his funeral but she also shared a fair amount of money with the grandchildren to assure that they could go to college. Truthfully, she kept very little money for herself. "Always pay yo bills and try to help yo family if you can." "Sometimes you can't give all yo money way foolin wit family cause they supposed to already have some too," she said. As far as the funeral was concerned, there was absolutely nothing shabby about it. Actually there was only a handful of people who attended the funeral, which is exactly how Joe would have preferred it.

Lilly made sure he was buried in a very nice suit that she had previously bought. As a matter of fact, on two occasions the girls overheard the mortician make a comment that the suit and hat was definitely upscale and that he recognized the designer, Christian Dior. The mortician also mentioned that he himself had never owned a suit of that quality. By this time the suit was actually many years old, but quite frankly Lilly always made sure that Joe always wore the best, because she wanted him to look pretty natty, especially when he went to church.

It's easy to say, "I wouldn't do this, or I wouldn't do that" but until you're actually in a situation, it's very difficult to know what you would do. Sure on many occasions the girls were extremely frustrated with Lilly for enduring and for exposing them to such violence as well, but they had to accept that Lilly did what she thought was the right thing to do at the time and they now realized that her feelings of fear, shame and embarrassment definitely played a big role as well. It doesn't mean that Lilly or anyone else should or would have handled the situation that way; it simply means that's how she chose to handle her business. Lilly was magnanimous and always insisted "I aint gone let nobody or nothin keep me out of the Kingdom of God and I'm gone love everybody, just like God said."

Fortunately by the grace of God, Lilly was a survivor of domestic violence instead of a statistic. Historically it was very common for the man to be a very dominate force in the household. Nowadays it's no surprise to see women stand up to their husbands and demand to be treated with respect or leave the marriage. According to Lilly, everybody has some kind of Cross to bear "even if it aint nothin but somebody tryin to take yo money 'way from you." Obviously this was the Cross that she chose to bear.

On the other hand, Joe didn't ask to be born with mental illnesses or personality disorders and it's very likely that he would have chosen something less severe had he been given the opportunity. Denise once recalled him say, "nobody knows my pain," but he didn't know how to explain the origin of his problem. Nobody in the family had any idea that he had such severe problems because he looked physically fine. There were times that he must have felt like a total idiot, but didn't know what was happening inside his brain, or how to fix it. He was a poor, black, uneducated man that knew nothing about mental illnesses or medications, other than the fact that he didn't want to take any more than necessary. What he and everyone else knew for sure was that he had family, financial obligations, etc. that he tried to provide for at least to the best of his ability.

At least he's now getting the peace and rest that he so very much deserves. "I don't like to think of him as being dead, but instead, that he was lulled into a spiritually induced coma," said Carolyn. Lilly said, "God don't make no mistakes and God gives the toughest tasks to the strongest soldiers." Surely Joe must have been very courageous to accept such a difficult task, to go through life alienating and annihilating meaningful relationships. Maybe it's a bit presumptuous, but perhaps he really was a strong soldier to have withstood all the mental illnesses and personality disorders during his lifetime.

"You know, I wouldn't be the least bit surprised to find that God had assigned him as one of Heaven's most precious greeters," said Carolyn. "I'm convinced that underneath all those layers of personality disorders and mental illnesses, he was actually a very kind and humble man that loved God and his family," said Denise. Sometimes Lilly worries about his soul, "I sho hope he made the right rangements wit God," she said. Whenever she says that, the girls referred her to his wallet that they saved, which contained many scriptures and pictures of Jesus, Angels, etc. that he carried.

"Well, we all got to go one day, whether we meet up wit God or the devil ...but if we want to have a good time, we better be prepared to meet God," said Lilly. They assured her that he had made peace with God. A friend once said, "Everybody has a tac in their shoe, some people have to take it off right away, while other's can walk on it for a mile and never know it's there."

"It would behoove us all to learn to be quiet and pray to God for strength and wisdom to face whatever challenges that may lie ahead," said Carolyn.

"And while we are praying let us not forget to pray for each other; and for those of us that feel that we need not pray because everything seems to be going so well, my advice would be to just keep living because eventually we all get a turn," said Denise.

"Since nobody gets out of this world unscathed, let us not be so willing to indulge into what is considered as juicy gossip and forget that *everybody got feelins*, according to Lilly."

As far as the legal system is concerned, they were all in somewhat of a quandary. When Lilly originally reported Joe for domestic violence, both she and Carolyn tried to explain some of the bizarre behaviors that he exhibited.

They thought that since the Police officer wrote down all the information, there would have been some type of Psychiatric Evaluation. Unfortunately they were given no specific information, but they felt *he was just fine.*

They didn't know what to think, other than the fact that nobody wanted to take the time to look into the mental health issues because it would have cost money for an evaluation and treatment. Perhaps the judge thought Lilly had made the choice to live in such an abusive environment and she should have divorced him or filed a complaint a lot sooner if there were problems, which is true. Carolyn feels that no one really took note of Joe's behaviors until he became a resident of the nursing home and they had ample time to spend with him. The nursing staff actually thought they were providing us with original information, but we reiterated the fact that his behavior had always been that way.

Once again, they thought that finally someone would have to address his mental health issues and provide treatment, but not so. Later they were told by the nursing home staff and the Psychological Department at the hospital that Joe actually was receiving psych medications, but they had no effect.

Obviously mental disorders can be very difficult to manage even if the person is agreeable to medications, counseling, etc. which Joe certainly was not. More often than not, people don't like the side effects, they definitely don't want to experience the loss of libido, weight gain, the feeling of lack of control over their lives, nor do they want to experience the anxiety while the doctor tweaks their medicines.

On the other hand, the law states that one cannot be forced to take medications unless they are a danger to themselves or others. If it were against the law to make an ass of one self, which is what Joe constantly did, then both the girls felt that a large percentage of the population would be in jail and mandated to take some type of medication.

During times that Joe did break the law, it seemed that the Police only gave him verbal warnings. Basically nobody wanted to put the time or money into his psychological issues but even if they did, people with mental health issues have Constitutional Rights that cannot be violated and in some instances, this is a good thing. At the end of the day Lilly felt that Joe actually had lived a pretty good life. He had good physical health and the freedom to raise all the hell that he wanted until the end. He wasn't confined to the nursing home for the last few years of his life but actually this was probably for the best because it's quite possible that someone would have eventually physically hurt him or vice versa, as he continued to spiral out of control.

It is estimated that at least five percent of jail victims are diagnosed with BipD and also five percent are undiagnosed. Billions of dollars have been wasted over the years keeping these people in jail instead of diagnosing and treating them. If an individual is truly Bipolar and Manic then jail time isn't the answer for an effective treatment.

Chapter Sixteen

On the Lighter Side

Believe it or not Joe actually had some pretty interesting qualities. He also had a sense of humor that was rarely seen. He dearly loved to listen to Country Western Music and Christian music by Mahalia Jackson. He truly enjoyed a good fruit cake, a hot cup of instant coffee with Pet Milk, Lucky Strike Cigarettes, and Lottery tickets!! And Astrology.

For some reason he was very interested in any and everything that pertained to Nostradamos and his predictions. His favorite television shows were: the evening news with Walter Cronkite, Dukes of Hazard and Hee Haw. At that time the television only showed three channels so it wasn't too hard for him to make choices. Joe's most common statements were as follows: "You aint gone run my damn life."

Although Joe was adamant that nobody would be running his life, this never deterred Lilly from trying to help him make good decisions. Although in his case there seemed to be no shortage of bad decisions and there was simply no reasoning with him once an idea came to his mind.

"I might look like a fool, but I aint no fool."

If you continuously make bad decisions, you do tend to look pretty foolish, which is exactly what he did on most occasions.

"Yall betta quit cuttin up."

If Joe said these words, you better watch out, because he would probably be bringing out the belt very soon. Whatever we were doing, we stopped immediately!

"She tell every fart that let!"

This was Joe's way of saying that you couldn't keep a secret.

"Always get yo education even if it aint no jobs round, so when a job come up, at least you can go get it. If you ain't got no education, you can't even sign up fo the job."

Sometimes he said things that really made since and this was one of those few times that he did. He didn't have a lot of money to contribute, but he was always willing to cosign on the college loan application with the understanding that he was in no way, shape or form planning to pay back one penny of the money. During Carolyn's last year of college she decided to marry Bob, and Joe refused to cosign any more student loans. He said, "If you old enough to get married, then you old enough to get yo own money for college." She was shocked as she had no means of borrowing money without his signature. She went to Lilly who said, "Go head and just sign his name on that paper." Carolyn gladly forged his signature, and Joe never knew. Although Lilly and Carolyn often laughed about it, Carolyn made sure she repaid every penny of the loan.

"What ail you fool?"

Joe didn't know how to be empathetic and was really quite harsh at times. If he thought you had any kind of problem this is how he responded.

"You can just kiss me all over" and or "kiss my wrist" and or "suck my……."

If Joe didn't like what you said, and things weren't going his way, this is usually what he said before he stormed out of the room. Of course the girls were very hurt to hear him speak to their mother that way, but they knew better than to say a word. Lilly never hesitated to fire back and inform him that she had no intentions of doing either of the three.

"I wish these people would go back home and take their asses to bed."

Joe absolutely hated people that drove real slow. He simply had no patience and honestly felt that they should go back to bed and start over. Perhaps he did have a point??

"A hard head make a soft ass."

Neither of the girls never really understood what Joe meant by this, but he sure said it a lot. Perhaps it was along the lines of …if you make your bed hard, then you'll have to lay on it and or if you make a bad decision, then you'll suffer the consequences. He had no problem letting them learn from their mistakes. If they thought he would bail them out of a mess, they were sadly mistaken.

"You aint grown til you can pay ALL YO OWN damn bills!"

Joe cared less about the legal age of eighteen. Unless you were actually paying for the total cost of all of your bills, then you better sit down and shut up, especially if you knew what was good for you as far as he was concerned. Not only did the girls have to sit down and shut up, their facial expressions better not appear as if they were upset. In his opinion, you were not entitled to the respect of an adult and he wasn't about to give it to you. The fact that you were an adult didn't mean a hill of beans to him. Of course he didn't respect Lilly too much either.

"Okee dokee or auight."

Joe never said yes or no, it was always okee dokee or auight.

"You aint got no time to pick no flowers" or "you betta quit assin roun."

This was Joe's way of saying hurry up and stop wasting time.

"You betta dance to my music."

If Joe said this, then we knew we had to do it his way no matter what.

"These ol jealous asses" or "you ole jealous tramps."

If Joe didn't like you, or if you really didn't see things his way, most likely this was how he referred to you which seemed to include a lot of people.

"Nothin from nothin leave nothin."

According to Joe if you were already flat broke, then why not spend your last dollar trying to win the lottery. After all.... somebody's got to win, why not Joe???

"I'll tell you just what's on the menu."

Joe had no problem telling you exactly what he thought.

"You betta eat what you want while you young cause when you get old, a lot of this shit you just can't eat no more."

Although Joe had a very matter of fact way of phrasing things, Carolyn attests that this is true because as she got older she found that many foods no longer agreed with her as well. Joe developed diabetes and high blood pressure later in life and had to give up a lot of his favorite foods as well.

"If you go to a party, don't let nobody bring you no drink, go get yo own damn drink. And if you leave a drink settin on the table to go to the bathroom, dump it out when you get back 'cause some of these ole asses will poison and kill you."

Although Carolyn wasn't much of a party goer, Denise sure was. They both often heard lots of stories about drugs being put in drinks, date rape, etc. The few times that they did attend parties, they remembered exactly what Joe said.

"You got dat shit right."

Whatever you said, Joe agrees with you!

"Don't neva change a tire cause you might not jack it up right and the car might fall on you, just call somebody"

Fortunately, neither of the girls had too many flat tires, but when they did, they would either call family or use road service. At this point neither of them have any interest in learning how to change a tire.

"You will have to go furrin here cause I don't know"

Joe wasted no time telling you to go further than him or ask somebody else.

"Don't neva walk off yo job lesson you got nother one, let em fire you. After they fire you, den just go get you nother job."

Joe worked in a factory and had the support of a union. Like anyone else, he didn't always like his job, but he faithfully went to work until the factory closed. If there was trouble at work, he just kept right on going.

"When you drivin that car, don't let nobody blow you nowhere."

Sometimes the intersections were kind of busy and the people behind Joe would sometimes blow but he never paid any attention to them because he needed to make sure that it was safe for him to go. If they blew too many times, he didn't mind giving them a good cussin' out or sometimes he would even blow his horn too.

"Don't neva go through a yellow light too fast always drive where you can stop if you have to and don't trail them semi-trucks too close cause they spill grease and you might slide."

Joe thought it was best to use caution when driving. He was truly one of those side seat drivers that sometimes really irritated you but he did have a pretty good driving record.

"You gone catch hell when you leave here"

Joe knew that both of the girls were really anxious to leave home after they turned eighteen. As far as they were concerned, they didn't think things could get too much worse and if so then at least they would be free of listening and watching his violent behaviors. In his own way, he tried to prepare and discourage them from being in a hurry to leave home because he knew they would encounter difficulties that life would bring. He too caught hell coming into this world, and Lord knows he caught hell trying to leave as well. Job 14:1-3. "Man born of woman is of few days and full of trouble. He springs up like a flower and withers away, like a fleeting shadow, he does not endure. This pretty much summed up his life.

"You is gone get yo ass knocked off"

If Joe saw somebody walking in the middle of the street while he was driving he would often yell these words. It really irritated him when the pedestrians wouldn't walk on the sidewalk. To tell you the truth, it is rather irritating to see people walk in the street while watching the cars swerve around them almost to the point of going into oncoming traffic just to prevent an accident.

"You rockin' yo jaws"

This was Joe's way of saying "you are really enjoying your food."

"You betta start pushin yo plate back."

If Joe felt that you needed to lose weight this was his advice. Although it was not appreciated at the time, everyone thought this was excellent advice.

"Just stop eaten, you aint got to do all that walkin and joggin just to lose weight; just look at all them people in Africa, they aint walked nowhere, and look how skinny they is."

Obviously Joe didn't believe in exercising to lose weight, but instead just eating less.

"Either way you go, you gone have plenty company... now say that's a lie."

Referring to Heaven or Hell, Joe felt that you wouldn't be alone whichever way you went. He never said a lot about wanting to go to either place.

"The United States is big enough to hold me."

Joe never had any desire to visit other countries. He loved to watch the nightly news and he also kept up with the happenings in other countries, but that was as close as he ever wanted to be.

"These damn white people is gonna do what they wanna do til Jesus come back. They think this world belong to them."

There were times when Joe felt that he had been discriminated against and he had no problem letting everybody know how he felt. In his defense, he did grow up during in the South during the time of Segregation and he often spoke of his discriminatory experiences. Joe definitely had his share of faults, but neither of his family members could honestly say they ever saw him discriminate against anybody. Indeed, he said a lot of things at home behind closed doors, but he never mistreated anybody because of their race. Carolyn never told him, but she was always very proud of the way he handled himself when she informed him of her plan to marry a white person. He later told her that he was glad she married Bob who turned out to be a wonderful husband and a very loving father to their children. Bob always made sure that Carolyn and the children never went without anything they needed even if it meant that he would have to be the one to go lacking.

"You just like a pair of false teeth, I can't do wit you and I can't do without you"

Denise remembers Joe making this statement to her on one occasion. She's not sure what she had done but she thought it was kind of funny at the time.

"Dont neva let nobody run you out of yo own house."

Now Joe always kept his shot gun handy just in case he came across somebody that he thought would take advantage of him. He wanted everybody to know that there was only one boss in the house and of course it was him.

"Quit playin possum. Stop pretending to be asleep."

"Sometime you can rush yo time." Joe believed that everybody had a scheduled appointment to meet their maker, but also that anyone could expedite their date if they chose to do so. Joe was always one to give advice, even though he rarely wanted to accept anyone else's. "Dont neva let nobody run you off yo job cause you gotta pay yo bills too. If the boss man don't like you, let him fire you, but don't you neva walk off yo job unlesson you got nother one ... and fuck them people."

Many things can be said about Joe but somehow he managed to have an excellent work ethic. He didn't believe that you should ever become so upset that you quit your job just because of the fact that others may not like you or even treat you very well. As the girls recall, the rules of the house that he enforced were made very clear and you never quit a job unless you actually had another one. It didn't matter how menial the job or how much you hated it, you were not allowed to quit!

"I wish y'all would quit breakin my rest."

"You're making too much noise, and you better quiet down and let Joe sleep if you know what's good for you!"

"Shit on dat, shit."

"Apparently Joe definitely does not agree with you...whatever you said. Perhaps you better come again."

"Now you got to get up early in the mornin to outsmart me."

Joe's family certainly begged to differ. In fact they felt that this statement was the furthest thing from the truth. Based on a lot of bad decisions Joe made, you didn't need to get up at all to be smarter than him.

Chapter Seventeen

A Visit with Joe's Sibling

Carolyn had the opportunity to visit one of Joe's siblings after his death. Carolyn had never spent any time with this particular individual, but since Joe's death, she thought it might be nice to visit one of his siblings, especially upon request. She and her husband actually traveled quite a distance to see his sibling, but after spending one week vowed never to return. Carolyn was absolutely dumbfound when she finally realized that his sibling had the exact same personality disorders and mental illnesses. It didn't take long before she noticed that this individual seemed to talk nonstop, but really didn't think much of it because she thought it was because the sibling was just glad to see her.

Needless to say, at the end of each day, Carolyn was truly exhausted by the conversation. As time went on, she noticed that this particular individual enjoyed bragging about many past sexual relationships, money, the desire to physically abuse others, grandiose ideas, etc. Also there was also a constant pressure to get Carolyn to agree with whatever was being said at the time, which wasn't always what she wanted to do. Basically Carolyn is a pretty straight forward gal who doesn't believe in sugar coating anything. Well, the straw that broke the camel's back was the last day of the trip at a restaurant. As they all sat down to have lunch, his sibling constantly badgered and asked questions concerning the degree of Joe's violent behaviors, which was a touchy subject for both of them who had previously agreed that no comments would be made as it actually served no purpose and their time together was supposed to be a time for bonding instead of bringing up the past.

Although Carolyn tried to make the best of things, she couldn't help but think that this individual had a hidden agenda to try to sway her opinions, which just wasn't about to happen. The more questions asked, the more Carolyn continued to hold her ground and provide what she felt were firm but honest answers. Since Carolyn certainly was not about to lie for the sake of appeasing anybody, she totally failed to see that this person wanted her to verbally agree and see things from the opposite perspective, which would have meant that the magnitude of Joe's behaviors had actually never happened and that it was all Carolyn's imagination.

Well, once Carolyn began to understand which way the conversation seemed to be going, she too became angry as she thought about all the abuse that she, Denise and Lilly had endured… after all, they were the ones that were actually affected. Perhaps she should have remained silent, just as Lilly had done so many times, but instead she went against Lilly's advice, "The more you stir in the shit, the more it stinks." Honestly, she never saw it coming, but somehow the situation escalated beyond her control. All of a sudden, this individual stood up in the restaurant and started yelling, waving arms around, etc. As Carolyn looked into the eyes of this person all she saw was pure rage and anger. Of course by this time their table was the center of attention as everyone stared on, which was terribly embarrassing.

Needless to say lunch was over. Who could eat at a time like that? Although they proceeded to walk slowly out of the restaurant, Carolyn felt like running. To make matters worse, Carolyn tried to console this individual with a gentle touch on the shoulder and asked if everything was o.k.; but once again, she failed to realize just how angry the individual was, because she was quickly made aware that her physical touch was not wanted and she was shoved away with great force. All of a sudden Carolyn had a flashback of Joe's angry outburst, and physical attacks towards Lilly. She really thought this person would physically attack her as well.

At that point it was crystal clear that the mental illnesses were hereditary. As a child, Carolyn vaguely remembered hearing Lilly say that this relative had been somewhat hard to get along with, but she never went into any detail. Of course Lilly wasn't the kind of person to gossip or say much of anything bad about any of her in laws and for the most part, she had her hands full, just trying to take care of herself and her family, which certainly wasn't easy. From that day on, there was no communication, nor did Carolyn feel the need to keep in touch with this individual, simply because she just had no energy to go back down memory lane to revisit any of those dreadful uncomfortable issues.

Chapter Eighteen

Nellie's Thoughts

"You was born on April fool and you is a fool."

These were Nellie's famous words to Joe in response to a lot of the crazy things he did. As children, both Denise and Carolyn recall visiting Nellie only once in a while, probably because Joe wasn't the social type; nor was it very unusual for Joe to have a falling out with almost everyone he knew and Nellie was certainly no exception. The fact that they were first cousins made no difference to Joe. Now Nellie doesn't waste a lot of time mixing words, which is most likely why Joe couldn't tolerate too much of her. To tell you the truth, the girls get pretty tickled when Nellie starts talking and they can almost tell what she is thinking just by the way she's looking. Nellie definitely talks with her eyes, which is a good thing, but they don't think she realizes it!

Now Nellie knew Joe quite well as a child, since the two of them grew up in the same house. After Joe's parents divorced, his mother took him and his three sisters to live with his grandparents, and Nellie was already there with her mother. There was no way his mother could work and care for him and his three sisters independently. Since Nellie had a lot of history with Joe, she was able to provide some accurate information of his childhood. According to Nellie, Joe was very mischievous and always tattling on the other kids, in hopes that they would get in trouble; but when it was all said and done, he too "got his ass beat" right along with everyone else. Joe never seemed to learn how to keep a secret or realize that he would also get in trouble. Whenever Nellie knew there was a chance that she was gonna get a whippin, she put on as many layers of clothes as she could in attempt to soften the blow. Now that must have been quite comical to see!

As an adult, Nellie didn't spend a lot of time with Joe, but she knew that his mannerism was somewhat unordinary. She didn't know exactly what his problem was, but she knew that something just wasn't quite right. She too had some dealings with Joe that were kind of unusual. Many years ago, Joe's father passed away and Nellie asked if she could ride along with him and Lilly out of state to attend the funeral. While at the funeral, Joe became upset and insisted that she would have to leave her suitcases because he claimed there was no room in the trunk. Of course, Nellie thought he was crazy, as she had no intentions of leaving her clothes out of state, especially since there was no mention of this issue on the way down. Fortunately, another male relative was there and informed Joe that Nellie's suitcase would definitely be going back in the trunk just as they left. It was later determined that Joe wanted Nellie to pay him to bring her suitcases back to Michigan simply because he wanted to buy some peanuts.

Nellie gladly gave him some money for peanuts just to settle him down. Of course Nellie never wanted to share a ride with him again, which is of no surprise. Yes, Lilly was there, but actually had very little if anything to say. Lilly never told this story, but Nellie sure did. Lilly was probably just glad Joe was finally yelling at somebody else for a change and after all it was his cousin.

Currently, Nellie gets together with the girls as often as possible. She only lives about thirty minutes away from Joe's family and is an absolute joy to talk to according to Carolyn who loves to hear of her stories, especially since she knows them to be true. Denise is also fascinated by the fact that at the age of 84, Nellie still bowls every Friday night, walks to church on Sunday, drives around town independently, and has a very positive outlook on life. Both Carolyn and Denise hope they'll be as healthy and active as Nellie when they're her age.

Chapter Nineteen

The Dancing Leaf

A few days after Joe's death, Carolyn remembers being in the basement going through her file cabinet. She had her head down, as she was very intent on finding specific documents that were needed for his funeral. While looking in the drawer, she distinctly heard a very gentle thumping or rustling outside the window. At first she paid no attention as she thought it was just a squirrel or a bird, especially since it was a very calm and sunny day. Following a short pause she continued to hear this same noise. She was a bit curious, but not really interested in going over to the window to see what the noise was, so she continued to ignore it. Another short pause followed, and she looked up, turned toward the window and noticed a single leaf gently dancing in the window panes. The leaf quickly swayed from one pane to the next as if it was trying to get her attention. Carolyn couldn't believe it as she had never seen anything like it in the past. She stood in amazement and watched the leaf for about three minutes. She said out loud "Dad, I know it's you,"

Perhaps Joe may have been trying to let her know that he was alright or that indeed she made the right arrangements. She finally walked away and left the dancing leaf in the window. Afterwards she wondered if should have stayed to see just how long it would continue but she felt that the point was made. She has had no similar experiences since that day, but she was comforted each time she recalled that spiritual experience.

◇◇◇◇◇◇

Regardless of his past behavior, they all pined for his loss. Because love is so strong, it is affected by nothing, no abuse nor anything. It's very possible to be afraid of someone and even hate a person's behavior and yet still love them. It's really rather strange but true. Perhaps the only explanation is based upon Biblical scripture that clearly states that God loves unconditionally.

Jeremiah 31: 3 "I have loved you with an everlasting love; I have drawn you with loving kindness."

Not only did they grieve for the loss of Joe, but they also grieved for all the violence that occurred. When a child witnesses so many years of violence, it doesn't just go away because the person dies.

Because Carolyn had such a difficult time accepting things that happened, she wanted to know more about the scientific reasoning behind his behaviors. On the other hand, Lilly and Denise felt that they just needed to try to pick up the pieces and move on. Sure Carolyn could have opted to seek professional counseling by sitting and telling some stranger of her innermost thoughts and feelings, taking endless medications, etc., but instead she decided to study and gain some insight about the chemical process that took place inside his brain that caused him and everyone else such misery.

Meet Joe's Family – Photo Album

My father, Louis

My mother Willie Jewel attends funeral of their four month old daughter

My parents and sister, Linda

Family breakfast

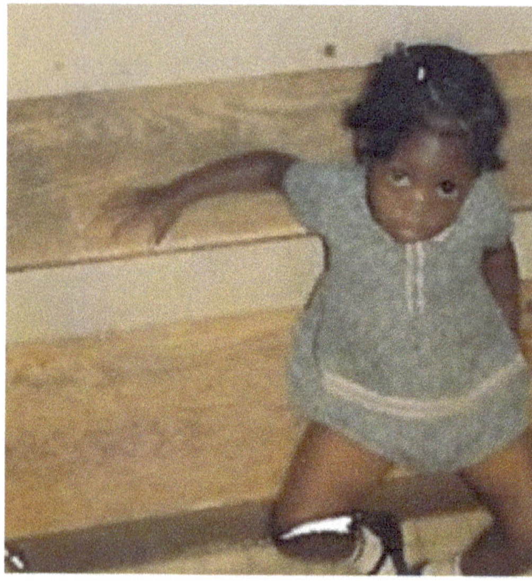

Gladys at age three

Grandma Elnora

Louis and Willie attend his father's funeral

James and Gladys Seedorf family photos

Willie Jewel, daughters, and grandchildren

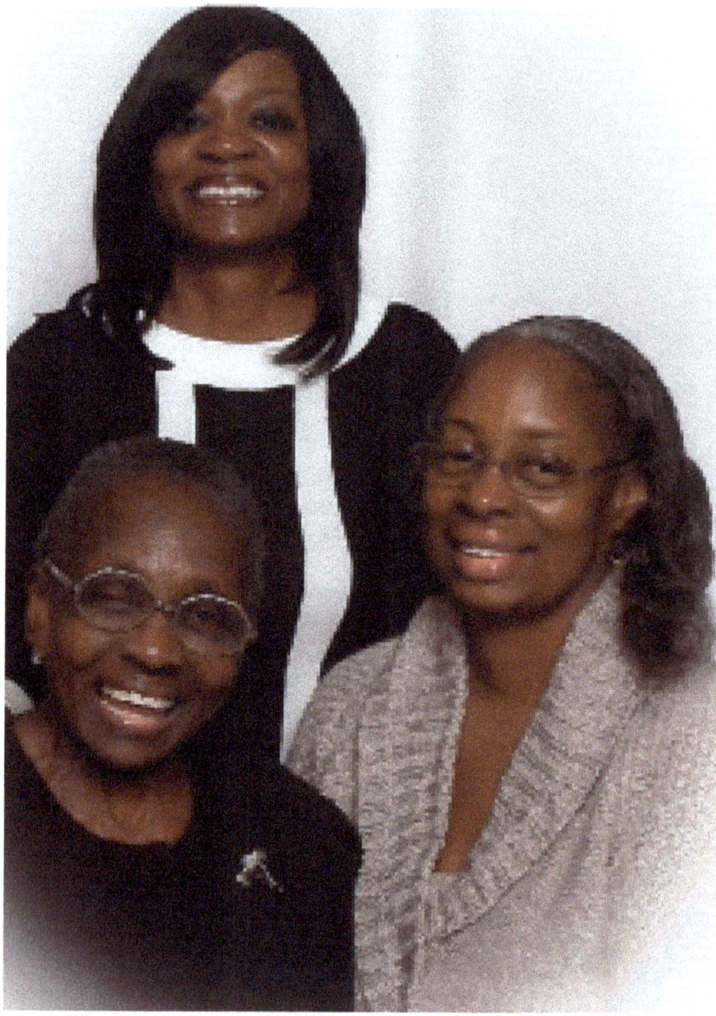

Willie Jewel with two daughters, Linda and Gladys

Louis's family photo

Part Two

Treatments Recommendations For Bipolar Disorders

Chapter Twenty

Bipolar Disorder, According to Dr. Jay Carter

In addition to reading as many books as she could get her hands on, she attended a very worthwhile seminar entitled: BIPOLAR: An Updated Slant on the Disorder-Including DSM-5, which was taught by Dr. Jay Carter.

Dr. Carter, Psy D., FPPR (Cand.), DABPS, is a licensed clinical psychologist and recognized national expert on Bipolar Disease (BiPD). He is a Diplomate Candidate in Psychopharmacology (FPPR Cand.) and is certified in Psychoactive Substance Abuse Disorders by the American Psychological Association. Dr. Carter has worked two and a half years as a Prison Psychologist and six years as a Psychologist at the Caron Foundation, which is one of the top three substance rehabs in the country. Dr. Carter has testified in local, state and federal court, as well. During his career, he has completed over 6,000 psychological and psychiatric evaluations. He spent two years evaluating children in the Wraparound Program to assess the strengths and needs of high risk children. Dr. Carter's experience comes not only from his clinical work, but also his personal life as well. Not only has he raised a daughter who is diagnosed as having BiPD, but was also raised by a mother who was also diagnosed with the disorder as well.

As Carolyn sat through the class and absorbed the information, tears came to her eyes because Dr. Carter's description of the Bipolar Disorder described Joe perfectly. Carolyn was astounded as she couldn't believe what she was hearing. If she didn't know better, she would have sworn that he knew Joe personally. The information that she learned was absolutely remarkable and lifted the fog on both the chemical and hormonal process that occurs with the Bipolar Disorder.

According to Dr. Carter, BiPD is not only a Spectrum Disorder but also a genetic and chemical disorder, rather than just a psychiatric illness. BiPD unbalances brain chemicals and as a result interferes with the person's ability to be or feel conscionable about anything, but yet be very cognizant everything. Individuals diagnosed with BiPD simply don't have the capacity to be conscionable which most take for granted. Ninety percent of the time, they are angry.

Let's say for example, that Joe went to the Dairy Queen to get ice cream; but as a result felt slighted and thus became angry because he had to wait in line longer than he thought was necessary. Instead of waiting patiently and realizing that perhaps there may be a staffing issue, he becomes fire mad and storms out the door, while pushing others out of the way and yelling at the person serving the ice cream. Unfortunately, it never occurred to Joe that the person serving the ice cream was more than likely overworked, underpaid and not to mention would also really like to have help serving the customers. By this time, the person serving the ice cream is obviously very hurt and embarrassed because there are now several customers staring and laughing out loud. Consequently, Joe is unable to imagine the person's hurt and embarrassment that he just caused because he doesn't have the capability of being conscionable.

The issue of the spectrum is vital regarding BiPD due to degree variations. On a scale of 1-10, Joe was a 10 meaning there was no chance of misdiagnosing his symptoms.

Specific information is as follows:

---

1 2 3 4 5 6 7 8 9 10

For instance, if an individual becomes nervous and talks a lot and even has trouble sleeping at night, they would most likely fall into the 1,2,3 category on the spectrum. At this point the individual may not be diagnosed as Bipolar because the issues in this category are very vague and are typically not diagnosed. Perhaps no symptoms may exist at this time. The next category is also not really diagnosable and is called the Soft Bipolar. This individual would fall within the range of 4, 5, 6; but may just be having some minor relationship issues. The third category BiPD, 7, 8, 9 may very well mean that the individual definitely has some mental issues, mood swings, and relationship problems. Symptoms are more pronounced. This particular category is very pronounced and causes great concern. The last category on the spectrum is BiPD10, which is most severe and is most certainly the section where Joe fit perfectly, in Carolyn's opinion. Joe exhibited extreme physical and verbal violence!

Temperament is absolutely essential in a BiPD and people with temperaments are prone to having BiPD. The idea of Temperament has not previously entered the conversation, but Dr. Carter states that it is now becoming a part of the discussion, at least in most psychological evaluations. Unfortunately very little research actually supports this theory, but Dr. Carter feels very strongly about it. Not all individuals have the same temperament, meaning that some of us are high strung and more aggressive than others while others are more passive. "Your temperament is the combination of inborn traits that subconsciously affect behavior. The traits are passed on by the genes. The alignment of temperament traits is just as unpredictable as the color of eyes, hair or size of body. Temperament makes a person introverted or extroverted and outgoing. Temperament makes one person creative in music or art and another interested in business, sports, or social events."[1]

Based on Dr. Carter's studies, ten percent of people diagnosed with BiPD have the GRK3 gene on Chromosome #22. This gene turns on, which is usually hormonal and stress induced and causes the individual to have a manic episode. During the manic episode, the individual feels that everyone else is talking in slow motion. All of a sudden the individual thinks faster and doesn't require as much sleep. Based on the night time violence that was witnessed, Joe had many manic episodes. Carolyn and Denise watched him take many short naps during the day while sitting up in the chair. Nevertheless, this was a great opportunity for them to change the channel on the television; however, once he woke up he was infuriated and said, "y'all done shit me right out of my show," and demanded that they never do it again or else!

Dr. Carter's clinical findings indicate that BiPD is also exacerbated by other things, such as hormones. For example, as a child, Joe recalled that his dad abruptly left the family unit, which may very well have caused his BiPD symptoms to be exacerbated or triggered. Drugs will also exacerbate BiPD as well, but when drug use is stopped, the BiPD goes away. It is not unusual to self-medicate with uppers and downers such as cocaine, alcohol, marijuana, etc. for the purpose of feeling better, not necessarily to get high. Statistics show that it's quite common for people with BiPD to self-medicate in attempt to manage their symptoms. On one hand, if the individual feels agitated and overwhelmed they may consume alcohol and or heroin to calm themselves. On the other hand if they feel down and depressed, they may use cocaine or some other drugs to lift their mood. Other than smoking cigarettes and caffeine (coffee, Coca-Cola) Joe did not use any drugs that anyone knew of.

Mania (mood swings, racing thoughts, agitation, etc.) may feel good to the individual but is dangerous, as it definitely causes a lack of sleep. Structured sleep is very important as it contributes to mania. It is not recommended that the individual with BiPD work unscheduled shifts, if possible. When a person is manic they don't see themselves in relation to anything. The individual also has an adrenal surge which is 2-3 times their normal strength. The loss of sleep causes a host of other problems such as delusional and psychotic thinking. The individual may also become paranoid, irritable and downright nasty! This is the time when bad decisions are made that can include: gambling, unprotected sex (insatiable sex drive), ruining relationships, nor do they recognize different levels of authority. It is unknown how long a manic period will last especially if no medication is taken. Needless to say, it's very hard to hold down a job.

Depression and possible thoughts of suicide always follows mania. 19.6 percent of people with BipD commit suicide when coming down from mania. The girls feel that Joe hardly ever came down from mania, which could possibly have kept him from committing suicide? After a manic episode, the person could have up to forty percent less serotonin in the brain. The lack of serotonin is associated with depression and hostility. It is during this stage that the individual may attempt to justify his or her actions.

Dr. Carter states that the scientific explanation for this behavior relates to the lack of brain development. Research states that the last part of the brain to develop is the Pre frontal lobe area which controls the ability to have insight, foresight, hindsight and the ability to realize the consequences of their actions. Development begins during the adolescence stage. Without the prefrontal lobe it is impossible to be aware of consequences and or to see that their actions are rude or hurtful to others. Fortunately the impact of the prefrontal lobe does not affect one's cognition or the ability to function or think, but it greatly impacts the ability to empathize with others. Executive functions such as reasoning or abstract thoughts don't exist which Joe's family definitely concurs.

Bipolar Manic Brain Dysfunction[2]

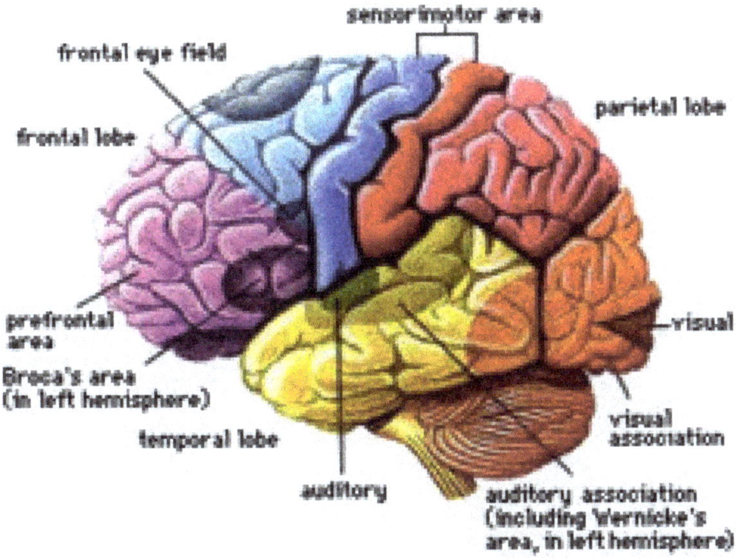

Trauma, hormones, and stress all tend to exacerbate BiPD. Based on Dr. Carter's findings, hormones have the greatest negative impact on BiPD than the others which explains why people tend to exhibit symptoms at the onset of Adolescence as this is the time the hormones are going crazy. Babies who carry the gene can have early onset if mother used substances when pregnant or if the child was traumatized in the womb. The next worst combination is bipolar and trauma. Traumatic events such as the death of a loved one, traumatic divorce, physical abuse, low self-esteem etc. all tend to exacerbate bipolar symptoms. Insomnia has also been known to exacerbate BiPD symptoms as well.

Manic behaviors in children can sometimes be misdiagnosed as an Attention Deficit Hyperactive Disorder. For instance if a BiPD child is put on Ritalin, it greatly exacerbates the symptoms. Caffeine, which is a Psycho stimulant can be a very dangerous substance for a child who is in a manic state because it could encourage either suicidal or homicidal symptoms.

Now Joe loved to drink regular coffee all day long which could very well explain some of his actions. Without fail each morning he started his day with a cup of coffee and ended the day with a cup of coffee as well. Basically Joe's life was a vicious cycle. It is assumed that Joe had BiPD at the onset of Adolescence, probably due to genetics and also many stressors that triggered the onset of his symptoms. Seventy five to eighty percent of the time he was in a manic state, which may be a slight exaggeration, but not much in Carolyn's opinion. Since he loved to drink coffee, which consequently added fuel to his already burning fire and unfortunately prevented him from sleeping at night since caffeine stays in the system for at least eight hours after being consumed. Due to the overload of stimulation he seemed eager to rock and roll while everyone else thought it was time to sleep!

Over a period of time such extensive sleep deprivation caused him to have delusions, paranoia, anger, psychosis, etc. With all the internal stimulation and lack of sleep, there was no way poor Joe could even begin to think of sleep, not even in his wildest dreams. It is quite possible that the steady flow of caffeine may have kept Joe stimulated enough to deter him from being depressed to the point where he would commit suicide. He would carry on for most of the night and then get up for work about five o'clock a.m. and immediately turn the coffee pot back on. By this time there was actually very little time for anyone else to get sleep before Carolyn or Denise had to get up and go to school the next morning. And the beat goes on and on. Somehow by the grace of God, he lived to be eighty years of age without killing himself or anyone else!

Research indicates that BiPD symptoms become worse over time, unless they are addressed. Mania manifests itself in four stages, according to Dr. Carter:

1. Adolescence begins around mid to late teens. During this stage the mania leaves the person feeling very good. At this point, the person has no idea that a problem exists; therefore, no assistance is sought. These feelings will go on approximately through the mid-twenties.
2. The next stage lasts from about the mid-twenties into the late thirties as the mania evolves to anger. The person doesn't feel quite as good, but still notices no problems; however, there is an ego arrogance and perhaps a feeling of entitlement that makes them feel good, as well. By this time the person would have a very difficult time managing the BiPD symptoms.
3. From the mid to late thirties into the early forties the individual tends to bounce from anger to anxiety and by this time problems are definitely noticeable. No doubt the person is having difficulty managing his/her life, relationships, etc. Sixty-three percent will wait until the illness is unmanageable before seeking help.

4. This last stage occurs between the age of fifty and into the sixties, which produce Schizoaffective symptoms. By this time, the individual is definitely unable to control his or her behavior.

Carolyn recalls that Joe walked perfectly through each stage, right up until the end. Had his name been Cinderella, the glass slipper would have been a perfect fit and Lord only knows who the wicked step sisters were.

The Diagnostic Statistical Manual Mental Health Disorders, which is used by psychiatrists, lists the symptoms that must be present in order to receive a diagnosis of BiPD.

The person must have at least one manic or hypomanic episode and have four to seven days of being abnormally high or angry.

Three of the next seven symptoms must be present consistently. It seemed that as Joe aged, he carried all symptoms at once:

- Big ego and a feeling of being the greatest in the world
- Insomnia, nor feel that they have no need to sleep
- Talking beyond their normal talkativeness
- Racing thoughts
- Easily distracted
- Hyper focused or goal oriented
- High risk behavior (extensive gambling, promiscuity, drug abuse)

Dr. Carter also feels that mood swings is another symptom.

The symptoms look differently in children who often present as being very irritable or bored, while adults tend to exhibit more depression and mania. It is not unusual for family members who actually live with the individual to find themselves very entangled in the tentacles of the BiPD to the point they would not recognize the symptoms.

The old saying, "You can't see the forest for the trees" was something Joe's family could attest to. There were many times that Joe's family felt that they had actually caused his anger, mood swings, etc. and blamed themselves. Much of their time was spent trying to stay out of his way. Lilly and the girls felt as though they were living in a fog. It really didn't occur to them that Joe had a disease, but eventually they suspected that something was wrong. If an individual feels that they did something wrong and somehow caused the physical or verbal abuse, then they're not so inclined to share that information with others because it draws even more negative attention to them, especially when they have someone standing over then saying, "What goes on in this house, stays in this house." BiPD is not only a roller coaster ride for the individual, but certainly for the family as well.

Treatment: (Information below is not a suggestion or recommendation for treatment)

Because the research is ever changing and new discoveries are constantly being made, it is highly recommended that the individual work closely with a psychiatrist. It is very important to remember that medications will not restore the prefrontal lobe, but instead present further mania.

Because the individual really has no idea what's happening inside the brain, treatment is not typically sought until they end up in court or the hospital. Some people are ashamed of their illness and won't seek treatment, but on the other hand, most are satisfied with the treatment received from their psychiatrist. If an individual decides that he or she doesn't care about hurting others and/or following doctor's instructions, then the prefrontal lobe will not develop. Like any other illness, he or she must first desire the mental health improvement. Also treatment involves not only medications, but also an adequate amount of sleep and very structured daily activities, good family involvement and support, etc. A pill alone is certainly not a nostrum, which is contrary to what most people believe.

Mood stabilizers, which may or may not be prescribed by the Psychiatrist are as follows:

- Lamotrigine/Lamictol (may be a good maintenance drug)
- Topiramate (Topomax)
- Gabapentine (Neurontin)
- Oxcarebaepine (Trileptal)
- Lithium has been known to reduce the rate of relapse and may also help prevent suicide. Some women can go off drugs while pregnant, but others may take temporarily while pregnant. Lithium is a natural salt that has been used for at least 150 years.
- Valproic Acid /Depakote - prevents cell death in the brain. Vitamin K may also be prescribed to assist in the prevention of conditions that may affect the unborn.

- Carbamazepine
- Zyprexia - will stabilize immediately, but may also increase appetite. Metformin may also be used in conjunction.
- Antipsychotics:
- Abilify- no weight gain
- Aripiprazole
- Olanzapine - side effects are not associated with birth defects, but is associated with weight gain, gestational diabetes, high blood pressure, etc.
- Aiprasidone
- Resperidone
- Invega
- Quetiapine (Seroquel) - could possibly cause drowsiness
- Clozapine
- Aserapine (Saphris)
- Haldol - not associated with birth defects
- Thorazien

Common Benzodiazpines/Anxiety:

- Lorzepam (Ativan)
- Clonazepam (Klonopin)
- Alprazolam (Xanex)
- Diazepam (Valium)

Electroconvulsive Therapy (ECT):

ECT - research states that ECT may pose fewer risks to fetuses. Complications are uncommon during pregnancy.

It's very important for pregnant women to stay well-nourished and hydrated while undergoing this procedure in order to prevent premature contractions.

Psychosocial Interventions:

- Psychotherapy
- Structured routine exercises
- Know early signs

Therapies:

1. Cognitive Behavior - Focuses on what precipitated the last episode by taking people into the frontal lobe and showing then the bigger picture as they don't go there too often. This is highly recommended by the National Institute for Mental Health and by WebMD.

2. Family Focused Therapy-The best intervention for mania is nurturing, touching, etc. Strong family bonds definitely out weigh Ego Arrogance.

3. Interpersonal Social Rhythm - focuses on lifestyle and the circadian rhythm.

4. Group Therapy—focuses on life goals.

5. Universal Intervention: This is a process which works almost every time.

    - Affinity - a willingness to be in the same space with the person

- Acknowledgement - not necessarily means that you agree with the individual

- Admiration-is the most valued of all three!

Natural Treatment for BiPD:

- Omega 3 Fish Oil
- Lithium Orotate
- Valerian (Kava Kava)
- Tryptophan (Turkey, raw milk, etc.)

A Holistic Approach

Each year Americans spend billions of dollars on natural supplements, vitamins, herbs, etc. and as a result holistic herbal medicine has proven to be an excellent means for mental health clients to address health issues without all the side effects of FDA approved medications. The Holistic approach does offer some very nice alternatives to treatment by bringing balance to the picture. Both traditional and holistic treatments are important and very nicely complement each other.

Jay Busemeyer, Stress Management Certified Trainer, provides his personal experiences, as he too is diagnosed with BiPD. As always, it is recommended that the advice of a doctor be sought before making any changes to medications.

According to Jay:

1. Regular exercise. After 20-30 minutes of exercise, endorphins are released and not only improve sleep, but also may decrease depression as well.

2. Meditation - even five or ten minutes per day promotes a greater awareness of oneself and also encourages the recognition of manic symptoms. Jay strongly suggest that anyone who struggles with BiPD should practice "mind fullness meditation", which is a tape that could be used in order to be more in tune with oneself. This meditation helps the individual focus on the here and now, calmness, etc. Since research has determined that BiPD is a result of having too much activity in a specific part of the brain called the amygdala and not enough in the prefrontal cortex, meditation can be very beneficial.

3. Reduction and or the elimination of sugar and caffeine. Both add fuel to the fire and do not help the mania! Green and white teas are much better for you and also filtered or bottled water is actually more important than drinking tea.

4. Omega 3 essential fatty acids, which reduces depression and irritability and may also aid in sleep. Omega 3 is cited for many other health benefits that include heart disease, cancer, arthritis, etc. For additional information, please go to the Omega Brite website.

5. Flower Therapy was first developed by Dr. Edward Back in the 1920's. Dr. Bach felt that people with different personalities could improve their health issues by responding to natural forms of therapy via flowers. Although flower essences do not cure illnesses, they do address emotional symptoms by allowing suppressed symptoms to surface. Since 1982 Dr. Bach's flower remedies have been used worldwide, which include

numerous flowers. Dr. Bach feel that disease is not just illness, but instead encompasses emotions, beliefs and life style, as well.

Eleuthero (Ginseng) root, Ginkgo or Rhodiola can be used for mental stimulation of the body's stress response, which are also referred to as Adaptagens. These are also good for someone that feels they are trapped inside one's body. Holy Basil is another source for reducing the stress response. "Licorice is another important herb in Traditional Chinese Medicine and is considered a balancer of the Five Organ Systems and has a synergistic effect on the other herbs in formula.[3] Nervines and Skullcap are also another important piece of the puzzle that seem to aids in calming the Central Nervous System.

6. Spiritual Healing - Asking for help and guidance via prayer, while on your journey is very essential to the healing process. Many people feel that healing can only occur on Sundays at church. Spiritual healing can occur anytime and anywhere as a result of spending time in the word of God, which also produces humility and is a good place to start with any overwhelming illness.
7. Staying away from stressful situations, getting enough sleep and having as much structure as possible are also very important in preventing an episode.
8. Support Groups - The key is to surround yourself with people that love and support you, and that you feel you can trust. People that you trust will always have your best interest at heart. The support of family and friends

is essential. Too much time spent alone can easily result in problems relating to unrealistic fantasies, depression, etc. One can never have enough loving family support.

9. Journal - Not everyone journals, but journaling could be a very useful way to manage thoughts, feelings, emotions, etc. By looking back at how much progress has been made as compared to your current status.

10. Awareness of Positive Thoughts or Belief - It always pays to be optimistic rather than pessimistic, regardless of the situation. A positive attitude determines the energy, time and effort that will be given to a task.

A quote from Sarah Young, (Jesus Calling Daily Devotional, (August 20) relates very nicely to this subject. It reads:

> *I am a God who heals. I heal broken bodies, broken minds, broken hearts, broken lives, and broken relationships. My very Presence has immense healing powers. You cannot live close to Me without experiencing some degree of healing. However, it is also true that you have not, because you ask not. You receive the healing that flows naturally from My Presence, whether you seek it or not. But there is more-much more-available to those who ask.*
>
> *The first step in receiving healing is to live ever so close to Me. The benefits of this practice are too numerous to list. As you grow more and more intimate with Me, I reveal My will to you more directly. When the time is right, I prompt you to ask for healing of some brokenness in you or in another person. The healing*

may be instantaneous, or it may be a process. That is up to Me. Your part is to trust Me fully and to thank Me for the restoration that has begun.

I rarely heal all the brokenness in a person's life. Even My servant Paul was told, "My grace is sufficient for you," when he sought healing for the thorn in his flesh.

Nonetheless, much healing is available to those whose lives are intimately interwoven with Mine.

Ask, and you will receive. Psalm 103:3; James 4:2; Corinthians 12:7-9; Matthew 7:7

Chapter Twenty-One

A Holistic Approach to Basic Nutrition and Basic Enzymes

Karla Anderson RN BSN LDHS LMT CNC CTTH of TRI CARE Holistic, specializes in digestive health and nutrition as well as neuromuscular integration therapeutic body work. Karla has at least sixteen years' experience in working with people who have mental illnesses and medical conditions. Since most diseases begin in the gut, Karla believes that it is essential to possess the adequate nutritional building blocks, which encourage wellness and prevention of the illness. As a result the chances of developing mental and medical symptoms will drastically diminish.

With regards to BiPD, if the proper nutritional building blocks are in place, there should be no mood swings, depression, sleeplessness, etc. Although Joe never met Karla, Carolyn tried to provide her with as much of Joe's medical history as possible. Karla then used the Loomis tool to determine Joe's medical findings. Carolyn was astonished with the results that were produced as she felt that the information that she received also described Joe pretty accurately. Based on the Loomis Digestive Health Assessment tool that was used, Karla was able to pinpoint all vitamin and nutritional deficiencies that may have contributed to Joe's behaviors. It was determined that Joe had moderate to severe issues with constipation, moderate inflammation, autonomic nervous system issues, endocrine/mid gastric issues as well. The findings indicated that Joe did not digest proteins or fats and as a result had issues with constipation, arthritis, anxiety, etc. Carolyn distinctly remembered that Joe frequently took laxatives as well as complained of having arthritis in the knees. Karla also explained that Joe's explosive anger issues were related to his high levels of Testosterone. The levels of Progesterone were directly related to his depression.

Based on the Holistic approach to basic nutrition, there are six daily building blocks that are needed to prevent illness:

1. Vitamins, water and fat soluble.
2. Minerals (Macronutrients or Mineral Nutrients (calcium, magnesium, potassium, sodium (acid) phosphorus, sulfur, chlorine. Minor minerals include iron, cobalt, copper, zinc, molybdenum, iodine, manganese and selenium.
3. Antioxidants Oxidation is a process that occurs in the body and produces free radicals which can be very damaging to the cells causing heart disease, cancer, and other diseases. Antioxidants are found in foods that destroy the free radicals that cause damage. Free

radicals can be caused by pollution, burnt foods, combustion, etc.

4. Essential Fatty Acids (Omega 3 & 6). Both are good for many issues such as inflammation and reducing blood pressure. May also aid in issues relating to diabetes, stroke, rheumatoid arthritis, asthma, inflammatory bowel disease, mental decline, etc. Omega 3 can be obtained from foods such as tuna, salmon, and mackerel. Dark green leafy vegetables and vegetable oils are also beneficial as well.

5. Digestive Enzymes. This is essential to the body to breakdown the foods that we eat. Three enzymes: Food, digestive and metabolic enzymes are necessary for getting nutrients moving.

   - Diabetes is linked to fat digestion and can cause constipation, gallbladder problems and heart disease.

   - Cancer is linked to protein digestion, which causes constipation, arthritis, anxiety attacks, etc.

   - Asthma is linked to carbohydrate digestion, which can cause diarrhea, fibromyalgia, and Attention Deficit Disorder.

6. Probiotics - Good bacteria that removes harmful toxins from the body and helps digestion.

During Joe's early sixties, he was diagnosed with type II diabetes. He was previously diagnosed with high blood pressure, arthritis and he was frequently plagued with canker sores and blisters in his mouth, especially in the winter. His diet was poor and as a result he was always constipated and frequently used laxatives. He also wasn't a fan of drinking water. It is pretty safe to say that his lack of building blocks may not have caused BiPD, but greatly contributed to it; however, there is "evidence that links many brain disorders, like Bipolarism to Mitochondrial cell injury from oxidative stress, which can be triggered by poor diet and nutrient deficiencies, toxins, infections, allergens, hormonal imbalances, altered gut function and stress (Hyman 2009).[4]

The Genetic Revolution in Biological Psychiatry research concludes that "genes guide the construction and composition of our brain cells, the connections between them, the neural network that arise as the brain develops, the chemical messengers enabling cell-to-cell communication, and the proper migration of neurons into functional brain centers and systems. As the orchestrator of our biological makeup, our genes contain instructions for making protein molecules - that is they carry the code for the building blocks of our mind and body.

In the brain, proteins organize themselves into neurons, and the neurons organize into specific neural networks controlling functional brain systems.[5] Unfortunately things can and do go wrong with the genetic process, which effects brain development. Research also suggests that there may be circumstances that involve the glutamate system that causes an increase in dopamine. Scientists are now looking for ways to reduce and control this process, which most likely causes psychosis and over stimulation. There are no specific blood test that are used to determine any specific form of mental illness, but the information may indicate if an individual would benefit from other forms of treatment.

Genetic research has determined that genes from a first degree relative impacts the possibility of mental illness in offspring.

No Genetic Relationship	Individual risk of obtaining Bipolar Disorder
Base Rate	1.2%
Brother or Sister	12%
One Bipolar Parent	27%
Both Bipolar Parents	74%
Identical Twins	74-80%

Source: E. Fuller Torrey, M.D., *Surviving Schizophrenia,* 5th Edition. NY: Collins Living, 2006.

Chapter Twenty-Two

Grass Roots

The Icarus Project, formed for the purpose of people that suffered with mental illnesses, was cofounded by Jacks McNamara in 2002 after being hospitalized only to find that she had been discharged with what she describes as unmet needs and a lack of support. Currently the Icarus Project is totally peer run and has over 15,000 members around the world.

Due to controversial issues, the project is sometimes referred to as the Recovery movement and or the Mad Pride. "The movement's goals: to redefine what it means to be sick for the 45.6 million American adults living with mental illness: develop a more collaborative treatment process between doctors and patients; make the public less fearful of people labeled mentally ill; and most important, de-stigmatize mental disorders for those who are diagnosed."[6]

Another well-known organization is the NAMI Family to Family Education Program (National Alliance on Mental Illness), which is the largest grass roots organization in the nation with over 1,100 affiliates. NAMI affiliates are engaged in several areas, such as advocacy, research, support and education while addressing mental illnesses: schizophrenia, bipolar disorder, obsessive compulsive disorder, panic disorder, post-traumatic stress disorder etc.

Carolyn attended a twelve week class taught by instructors and NAMI members: Virginia Haffner and Debbie Auton. Carolyn describes both of these instructors as her little angels who had a wealth of knowledge and also personal experience about mental illness, coping skills, advocacy, etc. By the end of the class, Carolyn felt that the knowledge she obtained, not only strengthened, but also confirmed the information she had previously obtained from other sources. She felt that the support and friendships that she formed during the class were as equally important as the information she received.

NAMI is available to individuals from all walks of life and is free of charge. It also takes into account the double stigma that certain groups such as lesbian, gay, bisexual, transgender (LGBT), people of color, etc., face every day by providing a very nonjudgmental and nonthreatening environment. "Research states that these people are likely to be at a higher risk for depression, anxiety and substance abuse disorders"[7] which is a direct result of prejudice and discrimination received from society. NAMI instructors provide all individuals with empathy and validation, while proactively presenting education and information that not only explains the illness, but eventually moves them into a position of advocacy. Advocacy also entails knowing the availability of services in the area, and that maneuvering the system, etc. is essential to helping the individual.

In attempt to improve the lives of individuals and families NAMI offers many classes and support groups that are very beneficial:

- *Family to Family* is a twelve week course that focuses on the emotional response of the family members.
- *NAMI Family Support Group Program* meets on a monthly basis and allows the individual and families to focus and discuss some of the challenges they face and how to cope as well. (May also be available in Spanish)
- *NAMI Basic* is a six week course that is mainly for parents and caregivers of individuals that perhaps have or have not yet been diagnosed with a mental illness.
- Peer-to-Peer is a ten week program offering education and support regarding recovery issues.
- NAMI Connection is a ninety minute weekly support group for individuals who suffer from mental illnesses to share and learn from each other and therefore gain a better understanding of the illness, etc.
- In Our Own Voice is open to the public to come and learn about mental illness and the many issues that are involved. The presentation attempts to cover the entire scope of mental illness while encouraging interaction of the members.

The benefits of the NAMI courses are endless. It offers hope to the hopeless, encouragement to the discouraged, understanding to those who feel misunderstood, most important a shoulder to cry on, and the list goes on and on.

There are approximately nine million people in Michigan. Approximately one of five individuals will be diagnosed with a mental illness; however, all is not lost. Mental illness is not a death sentence. There are many successful people who have led very happy and productive lives with the proper treatment and support: To name a few: Winston Churchill, Abraham Lincoln, Jane Pauley, etc. Greatness can still be achieved.

Endnotes

1. Jerry and Ramona Tuma and Tim LaHaye, *Smart Money*, Multnomah Books, 1994, p. 26.

2. Research (Dr. Amen) shows reduced prefrontal lobe activity during mania. Dr. Jay Carter, Bipolar, *The Elements of Bipolar Disorder.* Unicorn Press 2002 page 82

3. Julie Geldner, *Bipolarism: A More Holistic Approach,* Ohlone in Research Papers on June 22nd, 2010.

4. Julie Geldner. *Bipolarism: A More Holistic Approach.* Posted by Ohlone in Research Papers on June 22nd, 2010

5. E. Fuller Torrey M.D. *Surviving Schizophrenia*, 5th Edition. NY: Collins Living, 2006.

6. Alyssa Quart, oprah.com "A Saner Approach? New Ways of Treating Mental Illness." August 2013 issue of *O. The Oprah Magazine*

7 Joyce Burland, PhD. *NAMI Family-to-Family.* Double Stigma: GLBT People Living with Mental Illness. June 2007.

Bibliography

Anderson, Karla RN, BSN, LDHS, LMT, CNC, CTTH of TRI CARE Holistic.

Burland, Joyce Ph.D. NAMI Family-to -Family. 1977.

Bus Meyer, Jay, Stress Management Certified Trainer. Holistic Stress Relief. 2013.

Carter, Jay. Phyd. *DABPS Bipolar the Elements of Bipolar Disorder A Practical Guide*. Wyomissing, PA Unicorn Press 2002.

Carter, Jay. Psy D. *DABPS Bipolar: An Updated Slant on the Disorder*. Cross Country Education, 2013.

Geldner, Julie. *Bipolarism: A More Holistic Approach,* Online Herbal Center. Website by Computer Courage. 2009.

Quart, Alissa. A Saner Approach? New Ways of Treating Mental Illness. *The Oprah Magazine*, August 2013 Issue of O.

Torrey E. Fuller, M.D. *Surviving Schizophrenia*, 5th Edition., NY: Collins Living, 2006.

Townsley Cheryl N.D. *Discovering Wholeness.* The Spirit, Soul & Body Connection. Littleton, CO LFH Publishing 2000.

Young Sarah. *Jesus Calling 365 - Day Journaling Devotional* August 20. Nashville TN, Thomas Nelson 2008.

About the Author

Gladys J. Seedorf, LCSW was born in Cambridge, Maryland and raised in Albion, Michigan.

After graduating from Western Michigan University with a Master of Social Work Degree Gladys worked in several hospitals, hospice and home care agencies for the past twenty-four years providing services to homebound seniors and their families. Gladys is also very involved in the National Alliance for Mental Illness issues.

Gladys lives with her husband, two daughters and grandson in Battle Creek, Michigan. This is her second book.

Printed in the USA
CPSIA information can be obtained
at www.ICGtesting.com
CBHW060044231124
17755CB00012B/86

9 780989 259095